LOW-FAT
WAYS TO COOK
MEATS

LOW-FAT
WAYS TO COOK
MEATS

COMPILED AND EDITED BY
SUSAN M. MCINTOSH, M.S., R.D.

Oxmoor
House®

Copyright 1996 by Oxmoor House, Inc.
Book Division of Southern Progress Corporation
P.O. Box 2463, Birmingham, Alabama 35201

Library of Congress Catalog Number: 95-74601
ISBN: 0-8487-2205-1
Manufactured in the United States of America
First Printing 1996

Editor-in-Chief: Nancy Fitzpatrick Wyatt
Editorial Director, Special Interest Publications: Ann H. Harvey
Senior Foods Editor: Katherine M. Eakin
Senior Editor, Editorial Services: Olivia Kindig Wells
Art Director: James Boone

LOW-FAT WAYS TO COOK MEATS

Menu and Recipe Consultant: Susan McEwen McIntosh, M.S., R.D.
Assistant Editor: Kelly Hooper Troiano
Assistant Foods Editor: Kathryn L. Matuszak, R.D.
Copy Editor: Shari K. Wimberly
Editorial Assistant: Julie A. Cole
Indexer: Mary Ann Laurens
Assistant Art Director: Cynthia R. Cooper
Designer: Carol Damsky
Senior Photographer: Jim Bathie
Photographers: Howard L. Puckett, *Cooking Light* magazine;
  Ralph Anderson
Senior Photo Stylist: Kay E. Clarke
Photo Stylists: Cindy Manning Barr, *Cooking Light* magazine;
  Virginia R. Cravens
Production and Distribution Director: Phillip Lee
Associate Production Managers: Theresa L. Beste, Vanessa D. Cobbs
Production Coordinator: Marianne Jordan Wilson
Production Assistant: Valerie L. Heard

Our appreciation to the staff of *Cooking Light* magazine and to the Southern
Progress Corporation library staff for their contributions to this book.

Cover: *Grilled Sirloin with Roasted Corn Salsa (recipe on page 32)*
Frontispiece: *Pork Medaillons with Sweet Peppers (recipe on page 63)*

CONTENTS

MEATS PRIMER

*D*oes the sound of a juicy steak sizzling on the grill tempt
you to give up low-fat eating? You don't have to! With wise
shopping and low-fat cooking methods, you can freely enjoy
beef, veal, lamb, and pork. Read on to see how it's done.

The fact is, meat tastes good! Some people like it
so much that a meal without meat isn't really a
meal to them. And there is no doubt that meats do
contribute high-quality protein to the diet and are
good sources of vitamin B_{12}, niacin, zinc, and iron.

That's the good news. The bad news is that some
meats are high in cholesterol and fat, particularly
saturated fat that tends to raise levels of blood cholesterol. Yet health and nutrition experts still say
"yes" to meat. The trick is to start with lean cuts of
meat and use low-fat cooking techniques.

The recipes in this book have been developed to
help you accomplish that goal. They include only
the leaner cuts of meat and have little, if any,
added fat, thus keeping the percentage of calories
as fat around 30% or less for most recipes.

SELECTING LEAN CUTS OF MEAT

Preparing meat for a low-fat menu isn't difficult
at all if you choose the leanest cuts possible and
trim off any excess fat. The key to choosing lean
cuts of meat is to select those that have more muscle than fat. Also, look for cuts with the least
amount of marbling, or flecks of fat. (See chart on
page 10.)

In most recipes, 1 pound of boneless meat will
serve four, and 1 pound with bone will serve two to
three. As with all purchases, check the "sell by"
date and purchase the freshest product possible.
And make sure the meat looks and smells fresh.

*Lean cuts of meat have little marbling,
or streaks of fat.*

BEEF

The U.S. Department of Agriculture (USDA)
divides beef into three grades based on the fat content. Prime beef contains the most fat, which tenderizes the meat. It is usually available only to
restaurants, but you may find it in some larger
supermarkets.

Choice beef is the grade most often found in the
supermarket. Flecks of fat are evident in naturally
fatty cuts of choice beef like rib roasts, but naturally lean choice cuts can be low in fat. The leanest
cuts are those with the words "round" or "loin" in
the name. These include top round, top sirloin
steak, tenderloin, eye of round, and round tip.

Select is the leanest beef available to consumers.

Because select cuts are low in fat, they are much less tender, and they need extra attention such as marinating and moist cooking to tenderize them.

Beef should have bright red meat, and any fat it contains should be white. The meat should be fine-textured, firm, and slightly moist.

When purchasing ground beef, look for packages with the highest percentage of lean meat. Low-fat ground beef that is 95% lean will be a leaner choice than ground round (85% lean). Likewise, ground chuck (80% lean) will be leaner than ground beef (70% lean).

VEAL

Veal, one of the most delicately flavored meats, is very young beef. It is expensive in cost per pound, but most retail cuts have little waste. Good veal is pale pink in color. Redder meat indicates older, tougher veal.

Veal has little or no marbling and is therefore low in fat. The leanest cuts include the top round, leg cutlet, arm steak, sirloin steak, loin chop, and rib chop. It should be noted that even though veal is relatively low in saturated fat, it is higher in cholesterol than most lean cuts of beef.

LAMB

The distinctive taste of lamb offers variety and flavor to menus. Fortunately, sheep producers have answered consumers' requests for leaner meat. The leanest cuts include the word "loin" or "leg" in their names, as in leg of lamb and sirloin roast. As with other meats, trim all visible fat before cooking. Lamb has a cholesterol content similar to that of other meats.

Look for lamb with a bright pink color and pink bones. The redder the meat and bones, the older and tougher the meat.

PORK

Because pork producers have put their hogs on a diet, pork today is significantly lower in fat than in the past. Lean cuts of pork such as the tenderloin, loin chop, and top loin roast fit into a healthy eating plan. The amount of cholesterol in lean pork is about the same as that in lean beef.

When selecting pork, look for a bright pink color. However, always check the recommended sell-by date on the package to be assured that you are purchasing fresh meat.

Processed pork products are almost always high in fat and cholesterol. Regular bacon, sausage, cold cuts, and hot dogs contain too much saturated fat and cholesterol to be included in healthy meal plans. Many leaner versions of these items are available; check the nutrition labels to see what percentage of calories come from fat. Canadian bacon, which is actually cured and smoked pork tenderloin, is a processed pork product that is naturally very lean.

If sodium is a concern, avoid all cured and processed pork products.

WILD GAME

Buffalo and venison are available in some supermarkets, particularly in the western United States. Because of the active nature of wild game, it is lower in fat than most meats. However, the cholesterol content is similar to that of other red meats.

Many cooks are afraid to prepare game because it has the reputation of being tough and dry. Marinating and cooking by moist heat methods, such as braising or stewing, tenderize the meat and prevent it from drying out. As with other lean meats, overcooking toughens game.

STORING AND FREEZING

Place meat in the coldest part of your refrigerator as soon as possible after purchase. Prepackaged meat may be refrigerated unopened in its original wrapper—ground meat for 1 or 2 days and larger roasts and steaks for 2 to 4 days.

If you prefer, you may freeze prepackaged meat, without rewrapping, for up to 2 weeks. Or overwrap the original package with a moistureproof, vaporproof wrap such as freezer paper or aluminum foil. Overwrapped roasts and steaks will stay fresh in the freezer 6 to 12 months.

Freeze overwrapped ground meat or stew meat only 3 to 4 months. Leftover cooked meat may be frozen up to 3 months. When meats are frozen for longer than is recommended, they are more likely to lose flavor and moisture and develop an undesirable texture.

Thaw meat in the refrigerator in a plastic bag or in a dish so that juices do not drip onto other foods. Do not thaw meats in warm water or at room temperature to avoid the risk of food poisoning.

You may also defrost meat in the microwave oven; just follow your microwave oven manual for appropriate settings and times.

TENDERIZING MEAT

Marinate meats in fat-free or low-fat marinades to tenderize the meat and enhance the flavor. Acidic marinade ingredients such as wine, vinegar, and citrus juice soften the tough meat tissue.

For tenderizing, allow the meat to marinate at least 6 hours. Do not marinate for longer than 24 hours because the texture of the meat can break down too much. Always marinate in the refrigerator, not at room temperature.

Another way to tenderize meat is to pound it with a meat mallet. The butcher can run thin cuts of meat through a cubing machine to achieve the same result.

Commercial meat tenderizer, another possibility, is derived from tropical fruits that contain papain, a natural tenderizing agent. Follow package directions closely because meat can become mushy if too much tenderizer is used or if the tenderizer stays on the meat too long.

COOKING TO PERFECTION

The best method for cooking a piece of meat is determined by the tenderness of the cut. Tender cuts come from the rib, loin, and short loin sections, and include rib roasts, rib-eye steaks, and loin chops. They are usually more expensive and often higher in fat. Tender cuts may be cooked by dry-heat methods: broiling, grilling, pan-broiling, roasting, or stir-frying.

Less tender cuts of meat include round steak and roast, chuck roast, and flank steak. These usually do better when braised or stewed, which are moist-heat methods. To cook less tender meat by dry-heat methods, use one of the tenderizing techniques before cooking.

BRAISING AND STEWING

Braising is browning food and then cooking it, tightly covered, in a small amount of liquid at low heat for a long period of time. This can be done in the oven or on the cooktop. The long, slow cooking process tenderizes lean, less tender cuts of meat by breaking down the muscle fibers.

Stewing is similar to braising except more liquid is added and smaller pieces of meat are used.

Use vegetable cooking spray or a small amount of vegetable oil to coat the pan when browning the meat for braising or stewing. Refrigerate the braised meat or stew overnight to allow the fat that cooks out to congeal on the surface. Remove the congealed fat, and reheat.

The time required for braising or stewing can be decreased with the use of a pressure cooker. Today's pressure cooker is safer and easier to use than in years past. It can reduce cooking time by one-half to one-third for foods that require long, moist-heat cooking.

A pressure cooker speeds up the time needed for cooking lean cuts of meats.

BROILING AND GRILLING

When food is broiled or grilled, it is cooked directly under or over the heat source. Broiling is done in an oven, and grilling is done over hot coals or gas. Cooking temperatures are regulated by the distance between the food and the heat source. Tender cuts of meat are best for broiling and grilling.

During grilling, fat will cook out of the meat and drip onto the coals. To broil, place meat on the rack of a broiler pan to allow excess fat to drip away.

PAN-BROILING

For cooking thin, tender meat, pan-broiling is often faster and easier than regular broiling. It is also the process used for browning ground beef.

For pan-broiling, use a nonstick skillet or coat the skillet with vegetable cooking spray before adding the meat. Add little or no fat, and remove fat drippings as they accumulate in the skillet.

ROASTING

Roasting refers to cooking meat in an oven where the meat is surrounded by dry heat and develops a well-browned exterior and moist interior. Roasting usually works well for reasonably tender meats. Place the meat on a rack in a roasting pan so that fat drips away during cooking.

Oven-frying is similar to roasting except that the meat is usually breaded, and the result is much like a deep-fried meat but without the extra fat. Pork chops are often oven-fried.

STIR-FRYING AND SAUTÉING

These are two of the fastest cooking methods. For these techniques, cook food in a wok or skillet over high heat; stir the ingredients constantly so that they will cook evenly.

"TIMING" IT RIGHT

Because different cuts of meat vary in size and shape, suggested cooking times are not always accurate for a particular cut. We recommend the use of a meat thermometer to prevent over- or undercooking.

To use a meat thermometer, insert it at an angle into the thickest part of the meat. Make sure that the tip of the thermometer does not touch fat or bone. Keep the top of the thermometer as far away from the heating element as possible.

Meat continues to cook after it's removed from the heat source, so stop cooking when the thermometer registers about 5 degrees lower than the desired temperature. Make sure the temperature does rise the extra 5 degrees during standing time.

Bacteria is often present on the surface of whole cuts of meat. Cook steaks and roasts until at least the medium-rare stage to destroy the bacteria.

When meat is ground, bacteria may be spread throughout the meat. The rule for cooking ground meat is to cook it to the well-done stage so that no pink shows. Otherwise, bacteria present in the uncooked meat may not be destroyed and food poisoning may result.

USING LOW-FAT TECHNIQUES

Once you've purchased a lean cut of meat, don't add unnecessary fat during cooking. But even lean cuts of meat contain some fat that you can reduce by following selected techniques.

• Trim all visible fat from meat before cooking.

Use a sharp knife to trim away excess fat.

• Reduce or omit oil from marinade recipes and substitute water or broth.

• Use herbs, spices, and seasoning blends to flavor meats. Citrus juices, flavored vinegars, and wines can also help bring out the natural flavor of foods. If you season with salt or a seasoning that contains salt, do so after the meat is cooked because salting uncooked meat tends to draw out the juices.

• Cook with wine or other spirits to add flavor but not fat. Most of the alcohol and calories will evaporate during cooking, leaving only the flavor behind. If you don't have the wine or liqueur called for in a recipe, you can often substitute broth or fruit juice.

• Coat the grill rack with cooking spray before placing over hot coals to keep food from sticking.

• Roast or broil meat on a rack in a broiler pan so that fat is allowed to drip away. For easy cleanup, coat the rack and broiler pan with cooking spray before cooking, or you may line the pan (not the rack) with aluminum foil.

• Use a fat-skimmer to remove fat from meat drippings. Or chill meat drippings in the refrigerator to allow fat to harden and rise to the top. Skim off any solidified fat.

• Bake meat loaf in a loafpan with drain holes. The pan has a liner with holes that allow fat to drain into the outer pan away from the meat.

• Brown ground beef in a nonstick skillet without added fat or in a skillet coated with vegetable cooking spray.

• Spoon browned ground beef into a colander to drain excess fat. To further reduce fat, rinse with water.

A colander is useful for draining meat.   *Meat may also be drained on paper towels.*

• Reduce the fat content of cooked ground beef even more by patting it dry with paper towels after draining. If other ingredients are to be added to the skillet for further cooking, wipe drippings from the skillet with a paper towel.

COMPARISON OF NUTRITIONAL CONTENT OF MEATS

Cut (3 oz. cooked)	Calories	Fat (grams)
Beef		
Eye-of-round	156	5.5
Round Tip	162	6.4
Top round	162	5.3
Round	165	6.8
Tenderloin	173	7.9
Top loin	173	7.6
Sirloin	177	7.4
Flank	207	12.7
Ground beef, ultra-lean	146	7.0
Ground beef, extra-lean	218	13.9
Ground chuck	228	15.6
Ground beef	244	17.8
Veal		
Leg	128	2.9
Sirloin	143	5.3
Shoulder	145	5.6
Loin	149	5.9
Rib	151	6.3
Cutlets	185	10.5
Lamb		
Leg (shank half)	153	5.7
Leg (whole)	162	6.6
Sirloin	173	7.8
Shoulder	173	9.2
Loin	184	8.3
Rib	200	11.0
Pork		
Ham (lean, cured)	123	4.7
Tenderloin	141	4.1
Leg (whole, fresh ham)	188	9.0
Center loin	204	11.1
Loin	204	11.7
Shoulder	208	12.7
Wild Game		
Buffalo	111	1.5
Venison	134	2.7

LOW-FAT BASICS

*W*hether you are trying to lose or maintain weight, low-fat eating makes good sense. Research studies show that decreasing your fat intake reduces risks of heart disease, diabetes, and some types of cancer. The goal recommended by major health groups is an intake of 30 percent or less of total daily calories.

The *Low-Fat Ways To Cook* series gives you practical, delicious recipes along with realistic advice about low-fat cooking and eating. The recipes are lower in total fat than traditional recipes, and most provide less than 30 percent of calories from fat and less than 10 percent of calories from saturated fat.

If you have one high-fat item during a meal, you can balance it with low-fat choices for the rest of the day and still remain within the recommended percentage. For example, fat contributes 55 percent of the calories in Tossed Greens with Strawberries for the Quick-and-Easy menu on page 16. However, because the salad is combined with other low-fat foods, the total menu provides only 27 percent of calories as fat.

The goal of fat reduction need not be to eliminate all fat from your diet. In fact, a small amount of fat is needed to transport fat-soluble vitamins and maintain other normal body functions.

FIGURING THE FAT

The easiest way to achieve a diet with 30 percent or fewer of total calories from fat is to establish a daily "fat budget" based on the total number of calories you need each day. To estimate your daily calorie requirements, multiply your current weight by 15. Remember that this is only a rough guide because calorie requirements vary according to age, body size, and level of activity. To gain or lose 1 pound a week, add or subtract 500 calories a day. (A diet of fewer than 1,200 calories a day is not recommended unless medically supervised.)

Once you determine your personal daily caloric requirement, it's easy to figure the number of fat grams you should consume each day. These should equal or be lower than the number of fat grams indicated on the Daily Fat Limits chart.

DAILY FAT LIMITS		
Calories Per Day	30 Percent of Calories	Grams of Fat
1,200	360	40
1,500	450	50
1,800	540	60
2,000	600	67
2,200	660	73
2,500	750	83
2,800	840	93

NUTRITIONAL ANALYSIS

Each recipe in *Low-Fat Ways To Cook Meats* has been kitchen-tested by a staff of qualified home economists. Registered dietitians have determined the nutrient information using a computer system that analyzes every ingredient. These efforts ensure the success of each recipe and will help you fit these recipes into your own meal planning.

The nutrient grid that follows each recipe provides calories per serving and the percentage of calories from fat. In addition, the grid lists the grams of total fat, saturated fat, protein, and carbohydrate, and the milligrams of cholesterol and sodium per serving. The nutrient values are as accurate as possible and are based on the following assumptions.

• The calculations indicate that meat is trimmed of fat before cooking.

• Only the amount of marinade absorbed by the meat is calculated.

• When the recipe calls for cooked pasta, rice, or noodles, the analysis is based on cooking without additional salt or fat.

• Some of the alcohol calories evaporate during heating, and only those remaining are counted.

• When the recipe gives a range for an ingredient (3 to 3½ cups, for instance), the lesser amount is calculated.

• Fruits and vegetables listed in the ingredients are not peeled unless specified.

• Garnishes and other optional ingredients are not calculated.

Veal Steaks with Caper Sauce (menu on page 24)

SENSIBLE DINNERS

*I*s all this talk about keeping the percentage of calories from fat below 30 percent confusing? The following menus are designed to meet current dietary guidelines with no more than 30 percent of the total menu calories from fat. The low-fat entrées are accompanied by suggestions for side dishes and desserts in order to take the guesswork out of meal planning.

For a comforting evening at home, try the recipes for chili and coleslaw (page 15). If you need supper in a hurry, turn to the Quick-and-Easy menu on page 16. But when your calendar calls for elegant entertaining, go with the British-inspired menu on page 21, featuring Individual Beef Wellingtons.

Cold Weather Comfort

When the temperature starts to drop, nothing satisfies like a down-home bowl of chili. A robust mix of ground meat and vegetables, Chunky Beef-and-Vegetable Chili is composed of familiar ingredients. We've combined this spicy dish with two other all-time favorites: Colorful Coleslaw and Corn Muffins. (Our analysis includes one muffin and ½ cup orange segments per person.)

Chunky Beef-and-Vegetable Chili

Colorful Coleslaw

Corn Muffins

Fresh orange segments

Serves 8
Total Calories per Serving: 451
(Calories from Fat: 25%)

Chunky Beef-and-Vegetable Chili, Corn Muffins, and Colorful Coleslaw

CHUNKY BEEF-AND-VEGETABLE CHILI

¾ pound ground chuck
2 cups sliced fresh mushrooms
1 cup chopped onion
1 cup diced sweet yellow pepper
3 cloves garlic, crushed
2½ cups diced zucchini
1½ cups water
1 cup diced carrot
1 tablespoon sugar
2½ tablespoons chili powder
2½ teaspoons ground cumin
1½ teaspoons dried oregano
½ teaspoon salt
¼ teaspoon pepper
¼ teaspoon hot sauce
2 (16-ounce) cans kidney beans, drained
2 (14½-ounce) cans no-salt-added whole
    tomatoes, undrained and coarsely chopped
2 (8-ounce) cans no-salt-added tomato sauce

Cook first 5 ingredients in a large Dutch oven over medium-high heat until meat is browned, stirring until mixture crumbles.

Drain mixture, and return to pan. Add zucchini and remaining ingredients; bring to a boil. Partially cover, reduce heat, and simmer 1½ hours or until thickened, stirring occasionally. Yield: 8 (1½-cup) servings.

PER SERVING: 256 CALORIES (24% FROM FAT)
FAT 6.9G (SATURATED FAT 2.5G)
PROTEIN 16.8G   CARBOHYDRATE 34.2G
CHOLESTEROL 25MG   SODIUM 356MG

COLORFUL COLESLAW

⅓ cup reduced-fat mayonnaise
⅓ cup nonfat sour cream
¼ cup chopped fresh parsley
1 tablespoon sugar
½ teaspoon salt
¼ teaspoon ground ginger
2 teaspoons lemon juice
6 cups thinly sliced green cabbage
2 cups thinly sliced red cabbage
½ cup thinly sliced celery

Combine first 7 ingredients in a large bowl; stir until blended. Add green and red cabbage and celery; toss to coat. Cover and chill. Yield: 8 servings.

PER SERVING: 59 CALORIES (33% FROM FAT)
FAT 2.2G (SATURATED FAT 0.7G)
PROTEIN 1.7G   CARBOHYDRATE 8.6G
CHOLESTEROL 0MG   SODIUM 278MG

CORN MUFFINS

1 cup yellow cornmeal
1 cup all-purpose flour
2 teaspoons baking powder
¼ teaspoon baking soda
½ teaspoon salt
1 tablespoon sugar
1½ cups nonfat buttermilk
3 tablespoons vegetable oil
2 egg whites, lightly beaten
Vegetable cooking spray

Combine first 6 ingredients in a medium bowl; make a well in center of mixture. Combine buttermilk, oil, and egg whites; add to cornmeal mixture, stirring just until dry ingredients are moistened.

Spoon batter into muffin pans coated with cooking spray, filling three-fourths full. Bake at 425° for 12 to 14 minutes or until golden. Remove from pans immediately. Yield: 15 muffins.

PER MUFFIN: 105 CALORIES (28% FROM FAT)
FAT 3.3G (SATURATED FAT 0.6G)
PROTEIN 3.0G   CARBOHYDRATE 15.7G
CHOLESTEROL 1MG   SODIUM 165MG

QUICK-AND-EASY

This menu can be on the table in under 30 minutes—ready for family or guests. Assemble the ingredients ahead of time. While the chops broil, toss the salad and heat the peas and rolls. (The analysis includes two rolls per serving.)

Sweet-and-Savory Lamb Chops
Minted English Peas
Tossed Greens with Strawberries
Commercial hard rolls

Serves 4
TOTAL CALORIES PER SERVING: 539
(CALORIES FROM FAT: 27%)

SWEET-AND-SAVORY LAMB CHOPS

8 (3-ounce) lean lamb loin chops (1 inch thick)
2 cloves garlic, halved
1 tablespoon minced fresh rosemary
¼ teaspoon freshly ground pepper
Vegetable cooking spray
¼ cup honey
2 tablespoons stone ground mustard
Fresh rosemary sprigs (optional)

Trim fat from chops. Rub both sides of chops with cut side of garlic. Press rosemary and pepper evenly onto both sides of chops. Place on rack of a broiler pan coated with cooking spray. Combine honey and mustard; stir well, and set aside.

Broil chops 5½ inches from heat (with electric oven door partially opened) 6 minutes. Turn chops, and spread with honey mixture; broil 8 minutes or to desired degree of doneness. Garnish with rosemary sprigs, if desired. Yield: 4 servings.

PER SERVING: 259 CALORIES (31% FROM FAT)
FAT 8.9G (SATURATED FAT 3.0G)
PROTEIN 26.1G   CARBOHYDRATE 18.7G
CHOLESTEROL 81MG   SODIUM 214MG

MINTED ENGLISH PEAS

2½ cups frozen English peas
2 teaspoons minced fresh mint
1 teaspoon reduced-calorie margarine
¼ teaspoon salt

Place peas in a saucepan; add water to cover. Bring to a boil; reduce heat, and simmer 4 to 5 minutes or until peas are tender. Drain well. Add mint, margarine, and salt, stirring until margarine melts. Yield: 4 (½-cup) servings.

PER SERVING: 60 CALORIES (12% FROM FAT)
FAT 0.8G (SATURATED FAT 0.1G)
PROTEIN 3.7G   CARBOHYDRATE 10.1G
CHOLESTEROL 0MG   SODIUM 217MG

TOSSED GREENS WITH STRAWBERRIES

3 tablespoons unsweetened orange juice
2 tablespoons balsamic vinegar
1 teaspoon vegetable oil
2½ cups torn leaf lettuce
2 cups torn Bibb lettuce
1 cup sliced fresh strawberries
2 tablespoons thinly sliced green onions
1 tablespoon plus 1 teaspoon sesame seeds, toasted

Combine first 3 ingredients in a small bowl; stir well, and set aside.

Combine leaf and Bibb lettuces, strawberries, green onions, and sesame seeds in a large bowl; toss well. Pour orange juice mixture over lettuce mixture, and toss gently. Serve immediately. Yield: 4 (1½-cup) servings.

PER SERVING: 54 CALORIES (55% FROM FAT)
FAT 3.3G (SATURATED FAT 0.5G)
PROTEIN 1.7G   CARBOHYDRATE 5.4G
CHOLESTEROL 0MG   SODIUM 6MG

Sweet-and-Savory Lamb Chops and Minted English Peas

Oven-Barbecued Pork, Cornmeal Drop Biscuits, and Sautéed Kale and White Beans

DINNER IN THE NEW SOUTH

Although traditional Southern foods tend to be high in fat, you can still enjoy this region's recipes. Using updated cooking techniques and ingredients, we've lightened barbecued pork by starting with lean tenderloin. The high-fiber side dish is seasoned with herbs, not fat. Even with two biscuits per serving, total calories are under 500, with only 15 percent from fat.

Oven-Barbecued Pork

Sautéed Kale and White Beans

Cornmeal Drop Biscuits

Pineapple Mint Julep Sundaes

Orange Spice Tea

Serves 6
TOTAL CALORIES PER SERVING: 481
(CALORIES FROM FAT: 15%)

OVEN-BARBECUED PORK

2 (¾-pound) pork tenderloins
Vegetable cooking spray
2½ tablespoons no-salt-added ketchup
1½ tablespoons cider vinegar
1 tablespoon reduced-calorie maple syrup
2 teaspoons Dijon mustard
1 teaspoon low-sodium Worcestershire sauce
⅛ teaspoon ground red pepper
Fresh rosemary sprigs (optional)

Trim fat from tenderloins. Place tenderloins on a rack in a roasting pan coated with cooking spray.

Combine ketchup and next 5 ingredients; brush lightly over tenderloins. Insert a meat thermometer into thickest part of tenderloin. Bake, uncovered, at 400° for 30 minutes or until meat thermometer registers 160°, basting with remaining ketchup mixture. Let stand 10 minutes; slice diagonally across grain into thin slices. Garnish with rosemary sprigs, if desired. Yield: 6 servings.

PER SERVING: 152 CALORIES (25% FROM FAT)
FAT 4.3G (SATURATED FAT 1.4G)
PROTEIN 24.5G   CARBOHYDRATE 2.5G
CHOLESTEROL 79MG   SODIUM 113MG

SAUTÉED KALE AND WHITE BEANS

1 medium onion
Vegetable cooking spray
3½ cups chopped kale (about 5 ounces)
¼ cup water
1 cup canned cannellini beans, drained
½ cup chopped plum tomato
½ teaspoon dried rosemary, crushed
⅛ teaspoon salt

Slice onion, and separate into rings. Coat a large nonstick skillet with cooking spray; place over medium-high heat until hot. Add onion, and sauté 5 minutes or until tender.

Add kale and water to skillet; cover, reduce heat, and simmer 8 minutes or until kale is wilted, stirring often. Stir in beans and remaining ingredients. Cook, uncovered, over medium heat until thoroughly heated. Yield: 6 (½-cup) servings.

PER SERVING: 51 CALORIES (9% FROM FAT)
FAT 0.5G (SATURATED FAT 0.0G)
PROTEIN 2.6G   CARBOHYDRATE 9.5G
CHOLESTEROL 0MG   SODIUM 113MG

CORNMEAL DROP BISCUITS

1¼ cups all-purpose flour
⅓ cup yellow cornmeal
1½ teaspoons baking powder
¼ teaspoon salt
¼ teaspoon garlic powder
⅛ teaspoon ground red pepper
¼ cup chopped green onions
¼ cup plus 2 tablespoons skim milk
2 tablespoons vegetable oil
1 tablespoon honey
1 egg, lightly beaten
Vegetable cooking spray

Combine first 7 ingredients in a large bowl; make a well in center of mixture. Combine milk, oil, honey, and egg; add to dry ingredients, stirring just until dry ingredients are moistened.

Drop dough by heaping tablespoonfuls, 2 inches apart, onto baking sheets coated with cooking spray. Bake at 400° for 10 to 12 minutes or until lightly browned. Yield: 1 dozen.

PER BISCUIT: 98 CALORIES (28% FROM FAT)
FAT 3.0G (SATURATED FAT 0.6G)
PROTEIN 2.5G   CARBOHYDRATE 15.1G
CHOLESTEROL 19MG   SODIUM 97MG

Facts on Fiber

We've all heard that adults need to consume 25 to 30 grams of fiber daily. But how? Start with 5 servings of different fruits and vegetables. Then include a serving of high-fiber legumes nearly every day. Some popular legumes are cannellini beans (see Sautéed Kale and White Beans on page 19), kidney beans, split peas, black-eyed peas, and lentils. Finally, don't forget to have a serving of whole grains, cereal, bread, or pasta with every meal.

PINEAPPLE MINT JULEP SUNDAES

¾ cup unsweetened pineapple juice
1 tablespoon cornstarch
3 tablespoons bourbon
1 (8-ounce) can crushed pineapple in juice, drained
1 tablespoon minced fresh mint
3 cups vanilla nonfat frozen yogurt
Fresh mint sprigs (optional)

Combine pineapple juice and cornstarch in a small saucepan, stirring until smooth. Stir in bourbon, and cook over medium heat, stirring constantly, until mixture is thickened. Stir in crushed pineapple and minced mint; cook until thoroughly heated.

Scoop ½ cup frozen yogurt into each of 6 dessert dishes; top evenly with pineapple mixture. Garnish with mint sprigs, if desired. Serve immediately. Yield: 6 servings.

PER SERVING: 121 CALORIES (0% FROM FAT)
FAT 0.1G (SATURATED FAT 0.0G)
PROTEIN 3.6G   CARBOHYDRATE 27.9G
CHOLESTEROL 0MG   SODIUM 59MG

ORANGE SPICE TEA

¾ cup unsweetened orange juice
⅓ cup sugar
8 orange spice-flavored tea bags
2 (3-inch) sticks cinnamon
5½ cups boiling water

Combine first 4 ingredients in a large pitcher. Add boiling water; cover and steep 10 minutes. Remove and discard tea bags and cinnamon sticks; let cool. Serve over ice. Yield: 6 (1-cup) servings.

PER SERVING: 59 CALORIES (0% FROM FAT)
FAT 0.0G (SATURATED FAT 0.0G)
PROTEIN 0.2G   CARBOHYDRATE 14.9G
CHOLESTEROL 0MG   SODIUM 7MG

Individual Beef Wellingtons, Garlic Potatoes, and Lemon Broccoli and Tomatoes

A BRITISH AFFAIR

Plan a menu worthy of royalty with Individual Beef Wellingtons as the entrée. Serve Garlic Potatoes and an easy broccoli dish on the side, and then bring out the Steamed Pudding for dessert.

Individual Beef Wellingtons

Garlic Potatoes

Lemon Broccoli and Tomatoes

Green salad

Steamed Pudding

Serves 6
TOTAL CALORIES PER SERVING: 671
(CALORIES FROM FAT: 22%)

INDIVIDUAL BEEF WELLINGTONS

¾ pound fresh mushrooms, quartered
Butter-flavored vegetable cooking spray
¼ cup chopped shallots
2 cloves garlic, minced
2 teaspoons all-purpose flour
½ teaspoon dried marjoram
⅛ teaspoon pepper
1 (10½-ounce) can beef consommé, divided
2 tablespoons minced fresh parsley
6 (4-ounce) beef tenderloin steaks (1 inch thick)
1½ teaspoons low-sodium Worcestershire sauce
6 sheets frozen phyllo pastry, thawed
½ cup sweet Marsala
1 tablespoon plus 1½ teaspoons cornstarch

Position knife blade in food processor bowl; add mushrooms, and process until finely chopped.

Coat a large skillet with cooking spray; place over medium-high heat until hot. Add mushrooms, shallots, and garlic; sauté 2 minutes or until tender. Stir in flour, marjoram, and pepper. Gradually add ¼ cup consommé; stir well. Cook, stirring constantly, 5 minutes or until liquid evaporates. (Mixture will be thick.) Remove from heat, and stir in parsley; set mixture aside.

Trim fat from steaks. Coat a large skillet with cooking spray, and place over medium-high heat until hot. Add steaks, and cook 1½ minutes on each side or until browned. Drain on paper towels. Place steaks on a rack coated with cooking spray; place rack on a broiler pan. Drizzle ¼ teaspoon Worcestershire sauce over each steak; top each with 3 tablespoons mushroom mixture.

Working with 1 phyllo sheet at a time, lightly coat each sheet with cooking spray. Fold each sheet in half crosswise to form a 13- x 8½-inch rectangle; lightly coat with cooking spray. Fold each rectangle in half crosswise to form an 8½- x 6½-inch rectangle; lightly coat with cooking spray. Fold each rectangle in half crosswise to form a 6½- x 4¼-inch rectangle. Cut a ¼-inch strip from the short side of each rectangle; set aside. Drape phyllo rectangle over each steak, tucking edges of phyllo under steak. Lightly coat with cooking spray.

Crumple each ¼-inch phyllo strip into a ball; place on top of each phyllo-wrapped steak. Bake at 425° for 15 minutes or until desired degree of doneness.

Combine remaining consommé, wine, and cornstarch in a small saucepan; stir well. Bring to a boil, and cook, stirring constantly, 1 minute. Serve with steaks. Yield: 6 servings.

PER SERVING: 278 CALORIES (30% FROM FAT)
FAT 9.4G (SATURATED FAT 3.3G)
PROTEIN 29.0G   CARBOHYDRATE 18.3G
CHOLESTEROL 81MG   SODIUM 479MG

GARLIC POTATOES

1 small whole head garlic
½ cup water
1 tablespoon skim milk
1 tablespoon margarine, melted
2 tablespoons chopped fresh chives
1 teaspoon dried rosemary, crushed
¼ teaspoon salt
⅛ teaspoon pepper
18 unpeeled small round red potatoes (about 1½ pounds)

Remove white papery skin of garlic. Separate cloves; do not peel. Combine garlic cloves and water in a small saucepan; bring to a boil. Reduce heat, and simmer 15 minutes or until garlic is tender; drain and let cool 10 minutes. Peel garlic cloves, reserving garlic pulp; discard skins.

Position knife blade in food processor bowl; add garlic pulp, milk, and margarine. Process until well blended. Pour into a small bowl; stir in chives and next 3 ingredients.

Peel a ½-inch strip around center of each potato. Arrange potatoes in a vegetable steamer over boiling water. Cover and steam 25 minutes or until tender. Combine potatoes and garlic mixture in a bowl, tossing gently to coat. Yield: 6 servings.

PER SERVING: 124 CALORIES (16% FROM FAT)
FAT 2.1G (SATURATED FAT 0.4G)
PROTEIN 3.2G   CARBOHYDRATE 24.2G
CHOLESTEROL 0MG   SODIUM 130MG

LEMON BROCCOLI AND TOMATOES

1½ pounds fresh broccoli
1 cup cherry tomatoes, halved
1 teaspoon grated lemon rind
2 tablespoons fresh lemon juice
¼ teaspoon salt
⅛ teaspoon pepper

Trim off large leaves of broccoli, and remove tough ends of lower stalks; cut into spears.

Arrange broccoli in a steamer basket over boiling water. Cover, and steam 8 minutes or until crisp-tender. Place broccoli in a serving bowl; add tomato halves.

Combine lemon rind and remaining ingredients; stir well. Drizzle over broccoli mixture; toss gently. Yield: 6 servings.

PER SERVING: 37 CALORIES (12% FROM FAT)
FAT 0.5G (SATURATED FAT 0.1G)
PROTEIN 3.6G   CARBOHYDRATE 7.3G
CHOLESTEROL 0MG   SODIUM 130MG

STEAMED PUDDING

2 (1-ounce) slices French bread or other firm
   white bread, torn
1¼ cups all-purpose flour
½ teaspoon baking soda
¼ teaspoon salt
¾ teaspoon ground cinnamon
¼ teaspoon ground allspice
⅛ teaspoon ground mace
2 cups chopped dried pear
¾ cup raisins
¼ cup margarine, melted
¼ cup molasses
½ teaspoon grated orange rind
2 tablespoons unsweetened orange juice
1½ teaspoons vanilla extract
1 (8-ounce) carton plain low-fat yogurt
1 egg yolk
4 egg whites
Vegetable cooking spray
Whipped Cinnamon Sauce

Position blade in food processor bowl; add bread. Process 30 seconds or until bread becomes fine crumbs. Sprinkle crumbs on an ungreased baking sheet; bake at 250° for 7 minutes or until lightly browned. Combine crumbs, flour, and next 5 ingredients in a large bowl; stir well, and set aside.

Combine pear and next 8 ingredients in a bowl. Combine fruit and flour mixtures, stirring well.

Beat egg whites until stiff peaks form. Stir one-fourth of beaten egg whites into flour mixture; fold remaining egg whites into flour mixture. Spoon into a 6-cup metal mold coated with cooking spray. Cover tightly with aluminum foil.

Place mold on a shallow rack in a large stockpot; add boiling water to halfway up sides of mold. Cover and steam over boiling water 1½ hours, adding additional water as needed. Invert mold onto a serving platter; serve warm with Whipped Cinnamon Sauce. Yield: 16 servings.

WHIPPED CINNAMON SAUCE
1 cup 1% low-fat cottage cheese
¼ cup sifted powdered sugar
¼ teaspoon ground cinnamon

Position knife blade in food processor bowl; add all ingredients. Process until smooth. Yield: 1 cup.

PER SERVING: 201 CALORIES (17% FROM FAT)
FAT 3.9G (SATURATED FAT 1.0G)
PROTEIN 5.5G   CARBOHYDRATE 37.7G
CHOLESTEROL 15MG   SODIUM 215MG

Did You Know?

History tells us that classic Beef Wellington was named in honor of the first Duke of Wellington, a famous British soldier who defeated Napoleon at the Battle of Waterloo.

The dish calls for a whole tenderloin topped with pâté de foie gras (goose liver paste) and wrapped in puff pastry. In our rendition, a seasoned mushroom mixture and phyllo dough take the place of liver and pastry.

COMPANY'S COMING
(pictured on page 12)

This menu is perfectly suited for guests yet meets today's standards for fat and calories. Serve the veal with rice pilaf (½ cup each) and Balsamic Green Bean Salad. Make the salad several hours ahead to allow flavors to blend. Use commercial French bread if you don't have time to make your own. (Analysis reflects one slice per person.) A simple bowl of fruit sorbet (½ cup each) is recommended for dessert.

Veal Steaks with Caper Sauce

Commercial rice pilaf

Balsamic Green Bean Salad

French Bread

Fruit sorbet

Serves 4
TOTAL CALORIES PER SERVING: 518
(CALORIES FROM FAT: 17%)

VEAL STEAKS WITH CAPER SAUCE

2 tablespoons all-purpose flour
¼ teaspoon pepper
4 (4-ounce) boneless veal loin steaks (1 inch thick)
Vegetable cooking spray
1 teaspoon olive oil
½ cup canned no-salt-added beef broth, undiluted
1½ tablespoons capers
2 teaspoons Dijon mustard
½ cup nonfat sour cream
Fresh parsley sprigs (optional)

Combine flour and pepper; dredge veal steaks in flour mixture. Coat a large nonstick skillet with cooking spray; add oil. Place skillet over medium-high heat until hot. Add veal, and cook 2 minutes on each side or until browned. Remove veal from skillet. Drain and pat dry with paper towels. Wipe drippings from skillet with a paper towel. Return veal to skillet.

Combine beef broth, capers, and mustard; pour over veal. Bring to a boil; cover, reduce heat, and simmer 25 minutes or until veal is tender. Transfer veal to a serving platter, and keep warm.

Bring broth mixture to a boil; cook, uncovered, over medium heat 5 minutes or until mixture is reduced by about half. Remove from heat; add sour cream, stirring with a wire whisk. Spoon evenly over veal. Garnish with parsley sprigs, if desired. Yield: 4 servings.

PER SERVING: 186 CALORIES (27% FROM FAT)
FAT 5.5G (SATURATED FAT 1.3G)
PROTEIN 25.7G   CARBOHYDRATE 5.4G
CHOLESTEROL 91MG   SODIUM 438MG

Balsamic Green Bean Salad

1 pound fresh green beans
½ cup water
½ cup diced tomato
3 tablespoons balsamic vinegar
2 tablespoons grated Parmesan cheese
1 teaspoon anchovy paste
¼ teaspoon pepper
2 cloves garlic, minced
1 tablespoon pine nuts, toasted

Wash beans; trim ends, and remove strings.

Place ½ cup water in a large Dutch oven; bring to a boil. Add green beans; cover, reduce heat, and simmer 10 minutes or until crisp-tender. Plunge beans immediately into ice water for 5 minutes; drain. Place beans in a large bowl. Add tomato; toss well.

Combine vinegar and next 4 ingredients in a small bowl, stirring well. Pour vinegar mixture over vegetable mixture; toss gently. Cover and marinate in refrigerator at least 3 hours, stirring occasionally. Sprinkle with pine nuts just before serving. Serve with a slotted spoon. Yield: 4 servings.

PER SERVING: 71 CALORIES (30% FROM FAT)
FAT 2.4G (SATURATED FAT 0.7G)
PROTEIN 4.4G   CARBOHYDRATE 10.5G
CHOLESTEROL 2MG   SODIUM 228MG

French Bread

1¼ cups plus 2 tablespoons all-purpose flour,
    divided
1½ teaspoons rapid-rise yeast
1 teaspoon sugar
¼ teaspoon salt
⅓ cup hot water (120° to 130°)
¼ cup low-fat sour cream
1 teaspoon white vinegar
1 tablespoon all-purpose flour
Vegetable cooking spray
1 egg white
1 tablespoon water
½ teaspoon sesame seeds

Combine ½ cup flour, yeast, sugar, and salt in a medium bowl, stirring well. Gradually add water, sour cream, and vinegar to flour mixture, beating at low speed of an electric mixer until blended. Beat an additional 2 minutes at medium speed. Gradually stir in enough of the remaining ¾ cup plus 2 tablespoons flour to make a soft dough.

Sprinkle 1 tablespoon flour evenly over work surface. Turn dough out onto floured surface, and knead until smooth and elastic (about 8 minutes). Cover and let rest for 10 minutes.

Punch dough down, and knead lightly 4 or 5 times. Divide dough in half. Roll 1 portion of dough into a 4- x 5-inch rectangle. Roll up dough, starting at long side, pressing firmly to eliminate air pockets; pinch ends to seal. Place dough, seam side down, on a baking sheet coated with cooking spray. Repeat procedure with remaining dough. Cover and let rise in a warm place (85°), free from drafts, 20 minutes or until doubled in bulk.

Gently make 3 or 4 slits, about ¼ inch deep, diagonally across each loaf, using a sharp knife coated with cooking spray. Combine egg white and 1 tablespoon water; brush loaves with egg white mixture, and sprinkle with sesame seeds. Bake at 375° for 15 minutes or until loaves are golden and sound hollow when tapped. Remove from baking sheet, and let cool on a wire rack. Yield: 8 (1-inch) slices.

PER SLICE: 100 CALORIES (12% FROM FAT)
FAT 1.3G (SATURATED FAT 0.6G)
PROTEIN 3.3G   CARBOHYDRATE 18.4G
CHOLESTEROL 3MG   SODIUM 84MG

Calorie Alert

Can you really eat as much as you want as long as the food is low in fat? Unfortunately, the answer is no. Even low-fat foods contain calories, and you will gain weight when you eat more calories than you burn. It's important to monitor serving sizes, limit foods high in fat, and get plenty of exercise.

Sweet-and-Sour Pot Roast (recipe on page 30)

BACK TO BEEF

*B*eef continues to be a favorite American food. Now that we know more about lean cooking methods, it is easier than ever to include beef in low-fat menus. The first step is to choose the leanest cuts.

Suggestions for preparing lean beef tenderloin and eye-of-round roasts begin this chapter. Next are several recipes that call for lean steaks such as round and sirloin.

And what would a family do without ground beef? On page 41, you will find a basic meat loaf that calls for ground round. And on page 44 is a rich-tasting but low-fat lasagna.

Veal recipes begin on page 47. Veal, which is a very young beef, has a mild flavor appreciated by many. If cooking veal is new for you, try the Easy Veal Milano (page 51).

Beef Tenderloin au Poivre

BEEF TENDERLOIN AU POIVRE

1 (3-pound) beef tenderloin
3 tablespoons reduced-calorie margarine,
    divided
½ teaspoon whole white peppercorns, coarsely
    crushed
½ teaspoon whole green peppercorns, coarsely
    crushed
½ teaspoon whole black peppercorns, coarsely
    crushed
Vegetable cooking spray
12 small round red potatoes (about 3 pounds)
3 tablespoons water
2 tablespoons minced fresh chives
1 teaspoon coarsely ground pepper
½ teaspoon salt
3 tablespoons brandy

Trim fat from tenderloin. Combine 1½ teaspoons margarine and next 3 ingredients in a small
bowl, stirring well; rub peppercorn mixture evenly
over entire surface of tenderloin.

Place on a rack in a roasting pan coated with
cooking spray. Insert meat thermometer into thickest part of tenderloin, if desired.

Cut potatoes crosswise into ¼-inch slices, cutting
to but not through bottom of potatoes. Arrange
potatoes, cut side up, around tenderloin. Combine
remaining 2½ tablespoons margarine, water,
chives, pepper, and salt in a small bowl, stirring
well; brush potatoes evenly with half of mixture.

Bake tenderloin at 400° for 20 minutes. Reduce
heat to 375°, and bake an additional 35 to 40 minutes or until meat thermometer registers 145°
(medium-rare) or 160° (medium). Remove tenderloin from oven; transfer to a large serving platter.
Set aside, and keep warm.

Brush potatoes evenly with remaining half of
margarine mixture; bake an additional 15 to 17
minutes or until potatoes are tender and slices have
fanned out slightly.

Slice tenderloin diagonally across grain into ¼-inch slices; arrange potatoes around tenderloin.

Pour brandy into a small, long-handled saucepan; place over low heat just until warm (do not boil). Remove saucepan from heat. Ignite brandy with a long match, and pour evenly over tenderloin. Yield: 12 servings.

PER SERVING: 270 CALORIES (29% FROM FAT)
FAT 8.8G (SATURATED FAT 3.2G)
PROTEIN 25.9G CARBOHYDRATE 19.1G
CHOLESTEROL 69MG SODIUM 172MG

EYE-OF-ROUND ROAST WITH ONION SAUCE

1 (3-pound) eye-of-round roast
½ cup dry white wine
¼ cup white wine vinegar
1 tablespoon minced fresh parsley
1 teaspoon dried thyme
1 teaspoon dried rosemary, crushed
¼ teaspoon ground red pepper
1 clove garlic, minced
Vegetable cooking spray
2 cups water
2 large onions, thinly sliced and separated
    into rings
1 cup skim milk
1 tablespoon cornstarch
2 tablespoons Dijon mustard

Trim fat from roast. Place roast in a shallow dish. Combine wine and next 6 ingredients, stirring well. Pour mixture over roast. Cover and marinate in refrigerator 8 to 10 hours, turning occasionally.

Remove roast from marinade, reserving marinade. Place roast on a rack in a roasting pan coated with cooking spray. Insert meat thermometer into thickest part of roast. Pour water into roasting pan. Cover with aluminum foil, and bake at 450° for 20 minutes. Uncover and bake an additional 55 minutes or until meat thermometer registers 145° (medium-rare) or 160° (medium), basting roast frequently with marinade.

Let roast stand 15 minutes; cut diagonally across grain into thin slices. Transfer sliced meat to a serving platter, and keep warm.

Coat a Dutch oven with cooking spray; place over medium-high heat until hot. Add onion; cook 15 minutes or until tender, stirring frequently. Combine milk, cornstarch, and mustard, stirring until smooth. Gradually add milk mixture to onion, and cook over medium heat, stirring constantly, until thickened and bubbly. (Mixture will first appear curdled but will become smooth as it cooks.) Serve onion sauce with roast. Yield: 12 servings.

PER SERVING: 184 CALORIES (28% FROM FAT)
FAT 5.8G (SATURATED FAT 2.1G)
PROTEIN 25.3G CARBOHYDRATE 6.0G
CHOLESTEROL 57MG SODIUM 139MG

PICANTE POT ROAST

2 medium onions, cut into ¼-inch-thick slices
1 tablespoon chili powder
1 teaspoon sugar
1¼ teaspoons ground cumin
½ teaspoon dried oregano
¼ teaspoon ground red pepper
1 (4-pound) lean boneless bottom round roast
Vegetable cooking spray
1 (8-ounce) can no-salt-added tomato sauce
2 cups picante sauce
½ cup water

Combine first 6 ingredients in a medium bowl; toss well. Set aside.

Trim fat from roast. Coat a Dutch oven with cooking spray; place over medium-high heat until hot. Add roast; cook until browned on all sides. Combine tomato sauce, picante sauce, and water; pour over roast. Add onion mixture, and bring to a boil. Cover, reduce heat, and simmer 4½ to 5 hours or until roast is tender.

Transfer roast to a serving platter; serve with picante sauce mixture. Yield: 16 servings.

PER SERVING: 154 CALORIES (24% FROM FAT)
FAT 4.1G (SATURATED FAT 1.5G)
PROTEIN 22.9G CARBOHYDRATE 5.1G
CHOLESTEROL 56MG SODIUM 392MG

SWEET-AND-SOUR POT ROAST

(pictured on page 26)

1 (4-pound) lean boneless round-tip roast
Vegetable cooking spray
3 tablespoons brown sugar
½ teaspoon dry mustard
¼ teaspoon ground ginger
1½ cups unsweetened pineapple juice
½ cup cider vinegar
2 tablespoons low-sodium soy sauce
8 small carrots, scraped and cut into 2-inch
    pieces
8 small round red potatoes, scrubbed and
    halved
2 medium onions, quartered
¼ cup plus 1 tablespoon cornstarch
¼ cup plus 1 tablespoon water
Fresh parsley sprigs (optional)

Trim fat from roast. Coat a 4-quart pressure cooker with cooking spray; place over medium-high heat until hot. Add roast, and cook until browned on all sides. Remove roast, and pat dry with paper towels. Wipe drippings from pan with paper towels. Return roast to pressure cooker.

Combine brown sugar, mustard, and ginger; gradually add pineapple juice, vinegar, and soy sauce, stirring well. Add pineapple juice mixture to roast in pressure cooker.

Lock the pressure cooker lid; bring to high pressure over high heat. Adjust heat as necessary to maintain high pressure, and cook 30 minutes. Remove from heat, and let the pressure drop naturally (about 10 to 15 minutes). Remove the lid, tilting lid away to allow any excess steam to escape.

Add carrot and potato to pressure cooker. Lock lid, and return to high pressure over high heat. Adjust heat as necessary to maintain high pressure, and cook 5 minutes. Reduce pressure quickly by placing the pressure cooker under cold running water. Remove lid, tilting it away to allow excess steam to escape. Add onion. Lock lid, and return to high pressure. Cook 2 to 3 minutes. Reduce pressure quickly as directed above. Remove lid, tilting lid away to allow excess steam to escape.

Remove roast from pan, and place on a warm serving platter. Remove vegetables from juices with a slotted spoon, and arrange around roast.

Combine cornstarch and water; add to liquid in pressure cooker. Cook over medium heat, stirring constantly, until thickened. Serve gravy with roast. Garnish with parsley, if desired. Yield: 16 servings.

Note: To prepare roast by the conventional method, cook in a Dutch oven. Brown roast as directed above. Reduce pineapple juice to 1 cup and vinegar to ⅓ cup; combine and pour over roast as directed above. Cook roast, covered, in Dutch oven over medium-low heat 2 to 2½ hours, adding vegetables the last 45 minutes of cooking time. Decrease cornstarch to ¼ cup and thicken cooking juices as directed above.

PER SERVING: 214 CALORIES (24% FROM FAT)
FAT 5.8G (SATURATED FAT 2.1G)
PROTEIN 22.7G   CARBOHYDRATE 16.7G
CHOLESTEROL 61MG   SODIUM 110MG

FYI

When using a pressure cooker, follow these suggestions:

• Avoid overfilling the cooker. For most foods, fill the pan no more than two-thirds full. (Check manufacturer's instructions.) Overfilling can clog the vent pipe, resulting in a dangerous buildup of pressure.

• Check the valves and gaskets before using a pressure cooker, and make sure the vent pipe is clean. Lock the lid as directed so that the correct pressure can be reached.

• Remove the cooker from the heat at the end of the cooking time to let pressure drop slowly, or release the pressure quickly by placing the cooker under cold running water. Use the quick release method for foods that can easily overcook, such as vegetables.

• Remember that some steam remains even after all the pressure has been released. To avoid the risk of a steam burn, tilt the lid away from you when removing it.

Chili-Berry Steaks

CHILI-BERRY STEAKS

5 (4-ounce) beef tenderloin steaks
½ cup red wine vinegar
2 tablespoons low-sodium soy sauce
1 clove garlic, crushed
Vegetable cooking spray
¼ cup chili sauce
¼ cup seedless red raspberry jam
1 tablespoon sweet-hot mustard
1 tablespoon water

Trim fat from steaks. Combine vinegar, soy sauce, and garlic in a large heavy-duty, zip-top plastic bag.

Add steaks to bag; seal bag, and marinate in refrigerator 30 minutes, turning bag occasionally. Remove steaks from bag; discard marinade.

Coat grill rack with cooking spray; place on grill over medium-hot coals. Place steaks on rack, and grill 5 minutes on each side or to desired degree of doneness. Set aside, and keep warm.

Combine chili sauce and remaining ingredients in a small saucepan. Cook over medium-low heat until thoroughly heated, stirring occasionally. To serve, spoon sauce over steaks. Yield: 5 servings.

PER SERVING: 235 CALORIES (32% FROM FAT)
FAT 8.3G (SATURATED FAT 3.1G)
PROTEIN 24.6G   CARBOHYDRATE 14.5G
CHOLESTEROL 71MG   SODIUM 322MG

GRILLED SIRLOIN WITH ROASTED CORN SALSA
(pictured on cover)

1½ pounds lean boneless top sirloin steak
½ cup low-sodium soy sauce
¼ cup chopped green onions
2 tablespoons dark brown sugar
3 tablespoons fresh lime juice
⅛ teaspoon hot sauce
1 clove garlic, minced
Vegetable cooking spray
Roasted Corn Salsa
Fresh cilantro sprigs (optional)
Lemon slices (optional)
Orange slices (optional)

Trim fat from steak. Place steak in a shallow dish. Combine soy sauce and next 5 ingredients. Pour marinade over steak; turn steak to coat. Cover and marinate in refrigerator at least 2 hours; turn steak occasionally.

Remove steak from marinade; discard marinade. Coat grill rack with cooking spray; place on grill over medium-hot coals (350° to 400°). Place steak on rack; grill, covered, 5 to 6 minutes on each side or to desired degree of doneness. Let steak stand 5 minutes.

Cut steak diagonally across grain into thin slices; arrange on serving plates. Serve with Roasted Corn Salsa. If desired, garnish with cilantro and fruit slices. Yield: 6 servings.

ROASTED CORN SALSA
1 teaspoon vegetable oil
3 ears shucked fresh corn
Vegetable cooking spray
½ cup diced sweet red pepper
¼ cup finely chopped purple onion
2 tablespoons diced Anaheim pepper
2 tablespoons fresh lime juice
½ teaspoon vegetable oil
Dash of salt

Brush 1 teaspoon oil over corn. Coat grill rack with cooking spray; place on grill over medium-hot coals. Place corn on rack; grill 20 minutes, turning every 5 minutes. Let cool; cut corn from cob.

Combine corn, red pepper, and remaining ingredients in a bowl; stir well. Yield: 2⅓ cups.

Note: 1½ cups frozen whole-kernel corn, thawed and cooked, may be substituted for fresh, roasted corn, if desired.

PER SERVING: 224 CALORIES (32% FROM FAT)
FAT 7.8G (SATURATED FAT 2.6G)
PROTEIN 26.3G   CARBOHYDRATE 12.2G
CHOLESTEROL 73MG   SODIUM 158MG

SPICY SKILLET STEAKS

2 tablespoons cornmeal
¼ teaspoon garlic powder
¼ teaspoon ground cumin
¼ teaspoon dried oregano
⅛ teaspoon salt
⅛ teaspoon onion powder
⅛ teaspoon ground red pepper
4 (4-ounce) lean cubed sirloin steaks
Vegetable cooking spray
¼ cup plus 2 tablespoons no-salt-added tomato
    sauce
1 (4-ounce) can chopped green chiles, drained
1 large ripe tomato, cut into 16 wedges

Combine first 7 ingredients; stir well. Dredge steaks in cornmeal mixture. Coat a large nonstick skillet with cooking spray; place over medium heat until hot. Add steaks, and cook 5 minutes on each side or until browned.

Remove steaks from skillet. Drain and pat dry with paper towels. Wipe drippings from skillet with a paper towel.

Combine tomato sauce and chiles in skillet, stirring well; bring to a boil. Return steaks to skillet. Cover, reduce heat, and simmer 6 minutes or until steaks are tender. Add tomato wedges; cover and simmer 2 minutes or until thoroughly heated. Yield: 4 servings.

PER SERVING: 219 CALORIES (28% FROM FAT)
FAT 6.9G (SATURATED FAT 2.6G)
PROTEIN 28.6G   CARBOHYDRATE 9.5G
CHOLESTEROL 80MG   SODIUM 250MG

Spicy Skillet Steaks

Skillet Beef Burgundy

SKILLET BEEF BURGUNDY

1½ pounds lean boneless sirloin steak
Vegetable cooking spray
2 cups (½-inch) sliced carrot
2 cups quartered mushrooms
¾ cup coarsely chopped onion
1 pound small round red potatoes, peeled and
    quartered
1 teaspoon dried thyme
¼ teaspoon pepper
1 (10½-ounce) can beef consommé
3 tablespoons all-purpose flour
¾ cup dry red wine

Trim fat from steak. Cut the steak into 1-inch cubes. Coat a large nonstick skillet with cooking spray, and place over medium-high heat until hot. Add steak; cook 4 minutes or until steak loses its pink color. Remove steak from skillet; drain and set aside. Wipe drippings from pan with a paper towel.

Recoat skillet with cooking spray; place over medium-high heat until hot. Add carrot and next 3 ingredients; sauté 5 minutes. Return steak to skillet. Add thyme, pepper, and consommé; stir well. Cover, reduce heat, and simmer 30 minutes or until meat and vegetables are tender, stirring occasionally.

Combine flour and wine in a small bowl, blending with a wire whisk; add to steak mixture. Cook over medium heat, stirring constantly, 5 minutes or until thickened and bubbly. Yield: 5 (1½-cup) servings.

PER SERVING: 292 CALORIES (21% FROM FAT)
FAT 6.7G (SATURATED FAT 2.5G)
PROTEIN 31.5G   CARBOHYDRATE 25.5G
CHOLESTEROL 87MG   SODIUM 469MG

BEEF STROGANOFF

1 pound lean boneless sirloin steak
Vegetable cooking spray
3 cups sliced fresh mushrooms
¾ cup chopped onion
2 cloves garlic, crushed
¾ cup hot water
1 teaspoon beef-flavored bouillon granules
½ cup dry red wine
2 tablespoons all-purpose flour
1 tablespoon margarine
2 teaspoons low-sodium Worcestershire sauce
1 teaspoon dry mustard
½ teaspoon dried thyme
¼ teaspoon pepper
1 (8-ounce) carton nonfat sour cream
3 cups cooked medium egg noodles (cooked
    without salt or fat)
2 tablespoons sliced green onions

Partially freeze steak; trim fat from steak. Slice steak diagonally across grain into 2- x ¼-inch strips.

Coat a large nonstick skillet with cooking spray; place over medium-high heat until hot. Add steak, mushrooms, chopped onion, and garlic; cook 15 minutes or until steak and vegetables are tender. Drain steak mixture; set aside, and keep warm. Wipe drippings from skillet with a paper towel.

Combine water and bouillon granules in skillet. Combine wine and flour; stir well, and add to bouillon mixture. Stir in margarine and next 4 ingredients. Cook over medium heat, stirring constantly with a wire whisk, until thickened and bubbly. Add reserved steak mixture. Cook over medium heat until thoroughly heated. Remove from heat, and stir in sour cream. To serve, spoon steak mixture over noodles, and sprinkle with green onions.
Yield: 6 servings.

PER SERVING: 312 CALORIES (26% FROM FAT)
FAT 9.0G (SATURATED FAT 2.9G)
PROTEIN 26.6G   CARBOHYDRATE 28.9G
CHOLESTEROL 81MG   SODIUM 263MG

BEEF AND BEAN PICADILLO

1¼ pounds lean boneless top round steak
    (½ inch thick)
Vegetable cooking spray
1½ cups chopped onion
1 tablespoon seeded, chopped jalapeño pepper
2 cloves garlic, minced
3 cups water
1 (14½-ounce) can no-salt-added whole
    tomatoes, undrained and chopped
2 tablespoons dry red wine
1 teaspoon beef-flavored bouillon granules
½ teaspoon ground red pepper
½ teaspoon ground cinnamon
½ teaspoon ground cloves
¼ teaspoon ground allspice
1 (16-ounce) can black beans, drained
1 cup peeled, chopped apple
3 tablespoons raisins

Trim fat from steak; cut steak into 1-inch pieces. Coat a Dutch oven with cooking spray; place over medium-high heat until hot. Add steak; cook until browned on all sides, stirring often. Drain and pat dry with paper towels. Wipe drippings from pan with a paper towel.

Coat pan with cooking spray; place over medium-high heat until hot. Add onion, jalapeño pepper, and garlic; sauté until onion is tender.

Add steak, water, and next 7 ingredients, stirring well. Bring mixture to a boil; cover, reduce heat, and simmer 1 hour and 40 minutes. Add beans, apple, and raisins. Cover and simmer an additional 10 minutes or until steak and apple are tender.
Yield: 5 (1-cup) servings.

PER SERVING: 290 CALORIES (17% FROM FAT)
FAT 5.6G (SATURATED FAT 1.8G)
PROTEIN 31.4G   CARBOHYDRATE 29.1G
CHOLESTEROL 65MG   SODIUM 382MG

BEEF AND BROCCOLI STIR-FRY

1½ pounds lean boneless round steak
⅓ cup rice wine or dry white wine
3 tablespoons low-sodium soy sauce, divided
1 tablespoon cornstarch
3 tablespoons water
3 tablespoons honey
¼ teaspoon dried crushed red pepper
Vegetable cooking spray
2 teaspoons vegetable oil, divided
4 cups fresh broccoli flowerets

Partially freeze steak; trim fat from steak. Slice steak diagonally across grain into ¼-inch strips. Place in a heavy-duty, zip-top plastic bag. Combine wine, 2 tablespoons soy sauce, and cornstarch; pour over steak. Seal bag; shake until steak is coated. Marinate in refrigerator 2 hours.

Combine remaining 1 tablespoon soy sauce, water, honey, and red pepper; stir well, and set aside.

Coat a wok or large nonstick skillet with cooking spray; add 1 teaspoon oil. Heat at medium-high (375°) until hot. Add broccoli, and stir-fry 4 minutes. Remove broccoli from wok. Set aside, and keep warm.

Remove steak from marinade, reserving marinade. Add remaining 1 teaspoon oil to wok; heat wok at medium-high until hot. Add steak, and stir-fry 4 minutes or until done. Remove steak from wok; drain. Wipe drippings from wok.

Add steak, honey mixture, and marinade to wok; cook until thoroughly heated. Arrange broccoli on individual plates; top evenly with steak mixture. Yield: 6 servings.

PER SERVING: 230 CALORIES (27% FROM FAT)
FAT 7.0G (SATURATED FAT 2.1G)
PROTEIN 28.3G   CARBOHYDRATE 12.4G
CHOLESTEROL 71MG   SODIUM 260MG

BEEF TERIYAKI

1 (1½-pound) lean boneless sirloin steak
¼ cup water
¼ cup low-sodium soy sauce
2 tablespoons molasses
½ teaspoon ground ginger
2 cloves garlic, minced
Vegetable cooking spray
1 teaspoon vegetable oil
1 medium-size sweet red pepper, seeded and cut into strips
1 medium-size green pepper, seeded and cut into strips
½ cup sliced onion
1 cup sliced fresh mushrooms
1½ teaspoons cornstarch
4 cups cooked long-grain rice (cooked without salt or fat)

Partially freeze steak; trim fat from steak. Slice steak diagonally across grain into ¼-inch strips. Combine water and next 4 ingredients in a shallow dish; add steak to soy sauce mixture. Cover and marinate in refrigerator at least 1 hour. Drain, reserving marinade.

Coat a wok or large nonstick skillet with cooking spray; add oil. Heat at medium-high (375°) until hot. Add steak, peppers, and onion; stir-fry 5 minutes. Add mushrooms, and stir-fry 5 minutes.

Combine cornstarch and reserved marinade, stirring well; add to steak mixture. Cook, stirring constantly, until mixture is thickened and thoroughly heated. Serve steak mixture over cooked rice. Yield: 8 servings.

PER SERVING: 285 CALORIES (17% FROM FAT)
FAT 5.4G (SATURATED FAT 1.8G)
PROTEIN 21.5G   CARBOHYDRATE 35.3G
CHOLESTEROL 52MG   SODIUM 249MG

Indian Beef Kabobs with Corn

INDIAN BEEF KABOBS WITH CORN

⅓ cup water
⅓ cup mango chutney
1 teaspoon curry powder
½ teaspoon ground cardamom
½ teaspoon ground ginger
½ teaspoon ground cumin
¼ teaspoon sugar
¼ teaspoon pepper
⅛ teaspoon garlic powder
1 pound lean boneless sirloin steak
2 large ears fresh corn, each cut into 8
    (½-inch) pieces
1 large purple onion, cut into 8 wedges
Vegetable cooking spray

Place first 9 ingredients in container of an electric blender or food processor; cover and process until smooth. Set aside.

Trim fat from steak, and cut steak into 24 cubes. Combine steak cubes and chutney mixture in a large heavy-duty, zip-top plastic bag. Marinate in refrigerator 2 hours.

Remove steak from bag. Place marinade in a small saucepan, and bring to a boil; set aside.

Thread 6 steak cubes, 4 corn pieces, and 2 onion wedges alternately onto each of 4 (12-inch) skewers.

Coat grill rack with cooking spray; place on grill over medium-hot coals. Place kabobs on rack, and grill 6 minutes on each side or to desired degree of doneness, basting with reserved marinade. Yield: 4 servings.

PER SERVING: 292 CALORIES (23% FROM FAT)
FAT 7.4G (SATURATED FAT 2.7G)
PROTEIN 30.0G   CARBOHYDRATE 26.8G
CHOLESTEROL 82MG   SODIUM 114MG

Marinated Beef Kabobs

MARINATED BEEF KABOBS

1 pound top round or sirloin steak
½ cup red wine vinegar
¼ cup water
¼ cup low-sodium soy sauce
1½ teaspoons sugar
½ teaspoon dried thyme
½ teaspoon freshly ground pepper
1 clove garlic, crushed
8 medium-size fresh mushrooms
1 large yellow squash, sliced ½ inch thick
1 medium-size green pepper, seeded and cut into 1-inch pieces
Vegetable cooking spray
8 cherry tomatoes

Trim fat from steak; cut steak into 1½-inch pieces. Place steak in a heavy-duty, zip-top plastic bag. Combine vinegar and next 6 ingredients in a small bowl; stir well. Pour over steak; seal bag, and shake until steak is well coated. Marinate in refrigerator 4 to 8 hours, turning bag occasionally.

Remove steak from marinade. Place marinade in a small saucepan, and bring to a boil; set aside.

Thread steak, mushrooms, squash, and green pepper alternately onto 4 (15-inch) skewers. Coat vegetables with cooking spray.

Coat grill rack with cooking spray; place on grill over medium-hot coals (350° to 400°). Place kabobs on rack; grill, covered, 6 minutes on each side or to desired degree of doneness, basting frequently with marinade. Add tomatoes to skewers during last 1 minute of cooking. Yield: 4 servings.

PER SERVING: 198 CALORIES (28% FROM FAT)
FAT 6.2G (SATURATED FAT 2.0G)
PROTEIN 29.0G   CARBOHYDRATE 5.9G
CHOLESTEROL 73MG   SODIUM 179MG

Broiling Directions: Place kabobs on rack of a broiler pan coated with cooking spray; broil 5½ inches from heat (with electric oven door partially opened) 6 minutes on each side or to desired degree of doneness. Add tomatoes to skewers during last 1 minute of cooking.

GRILLED BEEF KABOBS

1 (1½-pound) lean boneless sirloin steak
½ cup commercial reduced-calorie Italian dressing
¼ cup dry red wine
12 boiling onions
12 large mushrooms
2 large sweet red peppers, seeded and cut into 1½-inch pieces
2 medium zucchini, cut into 1-inch pieces
Vegetable cooking spray

Trim fat from steak; cut steak into 1-inch pieces, and place in a heavy duty, zip-top plastic bag. Combine Italian dressing and wine; pour over steak. Seal bag, and marinate in refrigerator 8 hours, turning bag occasionally.

Cook onions in boiling water to cover 3 minutes; drain well, and set aside.

Remove steak from marinade. Place marinade in a small saucepan; bring to a boil. Reduce heat, and simmer 5 minutes. Set aside.

Thread steak, onions, mushrooms, pepper, and zucchini alternately onto 12 (12-inch) skewers. Coat grill rack with cooking spray, and place on grill over medium-hot coals. Place kabobs on rack, and grill 12 minutes or to desired degree of doneness, turning and basting frequently with marinade. Yield: 6 servings.

PER SERVING: 294 CALORIES (26% FROM FAT)
FAT 8.5G (SATURATED FAT 3.3G)
PROTEIN 30.8G   CARBOHYDRATE 23.9G
CHOLESTEROL 80MG   SODIUM 301MG

Cooking Tip

Tenderize meat for grilling by marinating it in any mixture with an acidic base, such as vinegar, fruit juice, or wine. Before using as a basting sauce, bring marinade to a boil and simmer 5 minutes. Baste meat frequently with the sauce while grilling.

Salisbury Steak

SALISBURY STEAK

If you use a regular skillet instead of a larger electric skillet, you may need to brown only half of the steaks at a time.

1½ pounds ground round
1 cup finely chopped onion
½ cup cooked long-grain rice (cooked without salt or fat)
¼ teaspoon pepper
1 egg white
Vegetable cooking spray
1¾ cups sliced fresh mushrooms
2 (13¾-ounce) cans no-salt-added beef broth
2 tablespoons Worcestershire sauce
½ teaspoon salt
2 tablespoons cornstarch
3 tablespoons water

Combine first 5 ingredients in a bowl; stir well. Divide into 6 equal portions, shaping each into a 1-inch-thick patty.

Coat an electric skillet with cooking spray; heat to 320°. Add patties, and cook 3 minutes on each side. Drain patties on paper towels; set aside, and keep warm.

Wipe drippings from skillet with paper towels. Recoat skillet with cooking spray. Add mushrooms, and cook at 375°, stirring constantly, for 3 minutes. Add broth, Worcestershire sauce, and salt; cook an additional 10 minutes, stirring occasionally. Return patties to skillet. Cover, reduce heat, and simmer 15 minutes. Transfer patties to a serving platter, and keep warm.

Combine cornstarch and water; add to broth mixture, stirring well. Bring to a boil; cook, stirring constantly, 1 minute. To serve, spoon sauce evenly over patties. Yield: 6 servings.

PER SERVING: 228 CALORIES (23% FROM FAT)
FAT 5.7G (SATURATED FAT 1.9G)
PROTEIN 29.0G   CARBOHYDRATE 11.9G
CHOLESTEROL 71MG   SODIUM 281MG

BAKED MEAT LOAF

1½ pounds ground round
1 cup chopped sweet red pepper
⅔ cup chopped onion
½ cup soft breadcrumbs
¼ cup no-salt-added tomato sauce
1 tablespoon prepared horseradish
½ teaspoon salt
¼ teaspoon black pepper
⅛ teaspoon ground red pepper
2 egg whites
Vegetable cooking spray
¼ cup reduced-calorie chili sauce
1 tablespoon sugar

Combine first 10 ingredients in a bowl; stir until well combined. Shape mixture into a 9- x 5-inch loaf, and place on the rack of a broiler pan coated with cooking spray. Bake at 350° for 35 minutes.

Combine chili sauce and sugar; stir well. Brush over meat loaf; bake an additional 15 minutes. Let stand 10 minutes before serving. Yield: 6 servings.

PER SERVING: 207 CALORIES (26% FROM FAT)
FAT 6.0G (SATURATED FAT 2.1G)
PROTEIN 27.0G   CARBOHYDRATE 9.8G
CHOLESTEROL 66MG   SODIUM 309MG

Fat Alert

Some butchers label ground beef as regular, lean, or extra-lean, while others label it hamburger, ground beef, ground chuck, ground sirloin, or ground round. Still others indicate the amount of fat in their products by stating the percentage of lean in their meat (for example, 85 percent lean ground beef).

Generally, ground round and ground sirloin are the leanest choices, followed by ground chuck and ground beef. Choose a ground beef with the highest percentage of lean to fat, such as ground round.

BEEF POT PIE

½ cup all-purpose flour
¼ cup instant nonfat dry milk powder
1 teaspoon dry mustard
1 cup water
1 tablespoon Worcestershire sauce
1 (10½-ounce) can beef broth
1 cup chopped onion
1 pound 93% ultra-lean ground beef
Vegetable cooking spray
1 tablespoon dried parsley flakes
½ teaspoon garlic powder
½ teaspoon pepper
¼ teaspoon dried thyme
1 (16-ounce) package frozen New England-
    style sweet peas, potatoes, and carrots,
    thawed
1 (6-ounce) jar sliced mushrooms, drained
1 (4.5-ounce) can refrigerated buttermilk
    biscuits

Combine the first 3 ingredients in a bowl; stir well. Gradually add water, Worcestershire sauce, and broth, stirring with a wire whisk until blended; set aside.

Cook onion and beef in a large saucepan coated with cooking spray over medium-high heat until browned, stirring until meat crumbles; drain in a colander. Return beef mixture to pan. Add parsley and next 5 ingredients; stir well. Add broth mixture; cook over medium heat, stirring constantly, 15 minutes or until thickened.

Spoon mixture into a 13- x 9- x 2-inch baking dish coated with cooking spray. Carefully split biscuits in half horizontally, and place over beef mixture. Bake at 400° for 10 minutes or until biscuits are lightly browned. Yield: 6 servings.

Note: You can assemble the casserole ahead of time, leaving vegetables frozen and omitting the biscuits; cover and freeze. Thaw frozen casserole overnight in refrigerator; let stand at room temperature 30 minutes. Top with biscuits; bake as directed.

PER SERVING: 293 CALORIES (21% FROM FAT)
FAT 6.8G (SATURATED FAT 2.1G)
PROTEIN 23.4G   CARBOHYDRATE 37.6G
CHOLESTEROL 59MG   SODIUM 778MG

GREEK MEATBALLS OVER RICE

1 pound ground round
½ cup soft whole wheat breadcrumbs
2 tablespoons finely chopped onion
2 tablespoons skim milk
1 tablespoon chopped fresh parsley
1 teaspoon minced fresh mint
1 teaspoon Worcestershire sauce
¼ teaspoon salt
¼ teaspoon pepper
1 egg white
1 clove garlic, minced
Vegetable cooking spray
2 (8-ounce) cans no-salt-added tomato sauce
2 tablespoons chopped fresh parsley
1 teaspoon dried oregano
¼ teaspoon sugar
¼ teaspoon pepper
3 cups cooked long-grain rice (cooked without
    salt or fat)

Combine first 11 ingredients in a medium bowl; stir well. Shape meat mixture into 30 (1¼-inch) meatballs.

Place meatballs on rack of a broiler pan coated with cooking spray. Broil 5½ inches from heat (with electric oven door partially opened) 8 to 10 minutes or until browned, turning after 6 minutes. Drain and pat dry with paper towels.

Combine tomato sauce and next 4 ingredients in a large skillet; bring to a boil. Add meatballs; cover, reduce heat, and simmer 10 minutes or until thoroughly heated. Serve over rice. Yield: 6 servings.

PER SERVING: 295 CALORIES (30% FROM FAT)
FAT 9.7G (SATURATED FAT 3.7G)
PROTEIN 19.4G   CARBOHYDRATE 32.3G
CHOLESTEROL 47MG   SODIUM 300MG

Greek Meatballs over Rice

Hearty Lasagna

HEARTY LASAGNA

Vegetable cooking spray
¾ pound ground round
1 cup chopped onion
3 garlic cloves, minced
¼ cup chopped fresh parsley, divided
1 (28-ounce) can whole tomatoes, undrained
1 (14½-ounce) can Italian-style stewed
    tomatoes, undrained and chopped
1 (8-ounce) can no-salt-added tomato sauce
1 (6-ounce) can tomato paste
2 teaspoons dried oregano
1 teaspoon dried basil
¼ teaspoon pepper
2 cups nonfat cottage cheese
½ cup freshly grated Parmesan cheese
1 (15-ounce) container nonfat ricotta cheese
1 egg white, lightly beaten
12 cooked lasagna noodles (cooked
    without salt or fat)
2 cups (8 ounces) shredded Italian
    provolone or mozzarella cheese, divided

Coat a large saucepan with cooking spray; place over medium heat until hot. Add meat, and cook until browned, stirring to crumble; drain and set aside. Wipe drippings from pan with a paper towel. Recoat pan with cooking spray; add onion and garlic, and sauté 5 minutes. Return meat to pan. Add 2 tablespoons parsley and next 7 ingredients; bring to a boil. Cover, reduce heat, and simmer 15 minutes. Uncover; simmer 20 minutes. Remove from heat.

Combine remaining 2 tablespoons parsley, cottage cheese, and next 3 ingredients in a bowl; stir well, and set aside.

Spread ¾ cup tomato mixture in bottom of a 13- x 9- x 2-inch baking dish coated with cooking spray. Arrange 4 noodles over tomato mixture; top with half of cottage cheese mixture, 2¼ cups tomato mixture, and ⅔ cup provolone cheese. Repeat layers, ending with noodles. Spread the remaining tomato mixture over noodles.

Cover and bake at 350° for 1 hour. Sprinkle lasagna with remaining ⅔ cup cheese; bake, uncovered, an additional 10 minutes. Let stand 10 minutes before serving. Yield: 9 servings.

PER SERVING: 380 CALORIES (25% FROM FAT)
FAT 10.5G (SATURATED FAT 5.7G)
PROTEIN 33.4G   CARBOHYDRATE 40.5G
CHOLESTEROL 50MG   SODIUM 703MG

TACORITOS

1 cup skim milk
1½ teaspoons chili powder
¼ teaspoon salt
⅛ teaspoon ground white pepper
1 clove garlic, minced
2 tablespoons cream of rice cereal, uncooked
1 tablespoon canned chopped green chiles
¼ teaspoon dried sage
¼ teaspoon dried oregano
¼ teaspoon ground cumin
Vegetable cooking spray
½ pound ground round
1½ cups chopped iceberg lettuce
1 cup seeded, chopped tomato
½ cup diced onion
1 cup (4 ounces) shredded reduced-fat
    Cheddar cheese, divided
8 (6-inch) flour tortillas

Combine first 5 ingredients in a medium saucepan; place over medium-high heat. Bring to a boil, stirring constantly. Add cereal; cook, stirring constantly, 1 minute. Transfer cereal mixture to container of an electric blender; cover and process until smooth. Combine cereal mixture, chiles, sage, oregano, and cumin in a medium bowl, stirring well; set mixture aside.

Coat a large nonstick skillet with cooking spray; place over medium-high heat until hot. Add beef, and cook until browned, stirring until it crumbles. Drain meat, and pat dry with paper towels.

Combine beef, lettuce, tomato, and onion in a large bowl; toss gently. Add ½ cup cheese and half of reserved cereal mixture; toss gently.

Spoon beef mixture evenly onto tortillas. Roll up tortillas, and secure with wooden picks. Place rolls, seam side up, in a 13- x 9- x 2-inch baking dish

coated with cooking spray; top with remaining cereal mixture.

Cover and bake at 350° for 10 minutes or until tortillas are thoroughly heated. Sprinkle with remaining ½ cup cheese; bake, uncovered, an additional 5 minutes or until cheese melts. Remove wooden picks before serving. Yield: 8 servings.

PER SERVING: 226 CALORIES (26% FROM FAT)
FAT 6.6G (SATURATED FAT 2.7G)
PROTEIN 14.9G   CARBOHYDRATE 28.8G
CHOLESTEROL 27MG   SODIUM 217MG

BEEF-STUFFED PEPPERS

1 cup frozen whole kernel corn
5 medium-size green peppers
Vegetable cooking spray
1 pound ground round
¼ cup chopped onion
½ cup (2 ounces) shredded reduced-fat sharp
    Cheddar cheese
⅓ cup reduced-calorie ketchup
1 teaspoon chili powder
1 teaspoon low-sodium Worcestershire sauce

Cook corn according to package directions, omitting salt and fat; drain and set aside.

Cut tops off peppers, and remove seeds. Chop tops; set aside. Cook peppers in boiling water 5 minutes. Drain peppers, and set aside.

Coat a large nonstick skillet with cooking spray; place over medium heat until hot. Add ground round, onion, and chopped pepper; cook until beef is browned and vegetables are tender, stirring until meat crumbles. Drain; pat dry with paper towels. Wipe drippings from skillet with a paper towel.

Return mixture to skillet; stir in corn, cheese, and remaining ingredients. Spoon mixture evenly into peppers; place peppers in a shallow baking dish. Add hot water to dish to a depth of ½ inch. Bake at 350° for 15 to 20 minutes or until thoroughly heated. Yield: 5 servings.

PER SERVING: 235 CALORIES (28% FROM FAT)
FAT 7.3G (SATURATED FAT 2.8G)
PROTEIN 27.0G   CARBOHYDRATE 15.8G
CHOLESTEROL 64MG   SODIUM 144MG

Beef and Bean Salad Olé

BEEF AND BEAN SALAD OLÉ

¼ cup plus 2 tablespoons mild salsa, divided
¼ cup white vinegar, divided
2 tablespoons water
4 (6-inch) corn tortillas
Vegetable cooking spray
½ pound ground round
½ teaspoon chili powder
¼ teaspoon dried oregano
1 (15-ounce) can dark red kidney beans, drained
½ cup chopped sweet yellow pepper
⅓ cup thinly sliced green onions
8 cherry tomatoes, quartered
3 cups torn iceberg lettuce
3 cups torn curly endive
¼ cup (1 ounce) shredded reduced-fat sharp Cheddar cheese

Combine 3 tablespoons salsa, 2 tablespoons vinegar, and water in a small jar; cover tightly, and shake vigorously to blend. Set aside.

Place tortillas on a baking sheet. Bake at 350° for 15 minutes or until crisp. Set aside.

Coat a nonstick skillet with cooking spray; place over medium heat until hot. Add beef, chili powder, and oregano; cook until meat is browned, stirring until it crumbles. Drain beef mixture; pat dry on paper towels.

Combine beef mixture, beans, and next 3 ingredients; toss gently. Stir in remaining 3 tablespoons salsa and remaining 2 tablespoons vinegar.

Place one tortilla on each of 4 salad plates. Divide lettuce and endive evenly among tortillas; spoon beef mixture evenly over lettuce. Top each with 1 tablespoon cheese; drizzle with salsa mixture. Yield: 4 servings.

PER SERVING: 254 CALORIES (23% FROM FAT)
FAT 6.6G (SATURATED FAT 2.2G)
PROTEIN 21.0G   CARBOHYDRATE 29.2G
CHOLESTEROL 40MG   SODIUM 358MG

VEAL SHANKS WITH SUN-DRIED TOMATO SAUCE

Serve this soul-satisfying dish with brown rice, steamed broccoli, and commercial multi-grain rolls for a low-fat, high-fiber meal.

4 (5-ounce) veal shanks
Vegetable cooking spray
1 teaspoon olive oil
1½ cups canned no-salt-added beef broth, undiluted
1¼ cups diced carrot
1¼ cups diced celery
1¼ cups diced onion
½ cup dry white wine
½ teaspoon dried basil
½ teaspoon dried thyme
¼ teaspoon salt
¼ teaspoon pepper
5 sun-dried tomatoes, quartered
3 cloves garlic, crushed
1 bay leaf
1 (15-ounce) can garbanzo beans, drained
⅓ cup minced fresh parsley

Trim fat from veal shanks. Coat a Dutch oven with cooking spray. Add oil; place over medium-high heat until hot. Add veal shanks, and cook until browned on all sides. Add beef broth and next 11 ingredients. Bring to a boil; cover, reduce heat, and simmer 2 hours.

Add garbanzo beans and parsley; cover and simmer an additional 10 minutes. Remove and discard bay leaf. Yield: 4 servings.

PER SERVING: 316 CALORIES (25% FROM FAT)
FAT 8.7G (SATURATED FAT 2.5G)
PROTEIN 27.9G   CARBOHYDRATE 31.2G
CHOLESTEROL 91MG   SODIUM 474MG

Veal Roast with Mushroom Sauce

VEAL ROAST WITH MUSHROOM SAUCE

1 (3-pound) boneless veal roast
½ cup brandy
¼ cup sherry vinegar
¼ cup minced shallot
1 tablespoon minced fresh parsley
1 teaspoon dried thyme
½ teaspoon freshly ground pepper
¼ teaspoon salt
1 clove garlic, minced
Vegetable cooking spray
2 cups water
Mushroom Sauce

Trim excess fat from roast. Place roast in a large heavy-duty, zip-top plastic bag. Combine brandy and next 7 ingredients in a small bowl; stir well. Pour brandy mixture over roast; seal bag, and shake until roast is well coated. Marinate roast in refrigerator 8 hours, turning bag occasionally.

Remove roast from marinade, reserving marinade. Place roast on a rack in a roasting pan coated with cooking spray. Insert meat thermometer into thickest part of roast. Pour water into roasting pan. Cover and bake at 325° for 1 hour and 25 minutes. Uncover and bake 1 hour or until meat thermometer registers 160° (medium), basting frequently with marinade.

Let roast stand 10 minutes; slice roast diagonally across grain into ¼-inch slices. Serve roast with Mushroom Sauce. Yield: 12 servings.

MUSHROOM SAUCE
Vegetable cooking spray
4 cups sliced fresh shiitake mushrooms
2 cups water
¼ cup all-purpose flour
2 teaspoons beef-flavored bouillon granules

Coat a large nonstick skillet with cooking spray; place over medium-high heat until hot. Add mushrooms; sauté until tender. Combine water, flour, and bouillon granules, stirring until smooth. Add flour mixture to skillet, stirring well. Bring to a boil; reduce heat, and simmer, stirring constantly, until thickened. Yield: 2½ cups.

PER SERVING: 200 CALORIES (25% FROM FAT)
FAT 5.5G (SATURATED FAT 1.5G)
PROTEIN 25.7G   CARBOHYDRATE 3.9G
CHOLESTEROL 92MG   SODIUM 307MG

ROSEMARY GRILLED VEAL CHOPS

6 (6-ounce) lean veal loin chops (¾ inch thick)
½ cup dry white wine
2 tablespoons lemon juice
2 teaspoons dried rosemary, crushed
¼ teaspoon pepper
⅛ teaspoon salt
4 cloves garlic, minced
Vegetable cooking spray

Trim fat from chops. Place chops in a heavy-duty, zip-top plastic bag. Combine wine and next 5 ingredients; stir well. Pour over chops; seal bag, and shake until chops are well coated. Marinate in refrigerator 2 to 4 hours, turning bag occasionally.

Remove chops from marinade. Place marinade in a small saucepan, and bring to a boil; set aside.

Coat grill rack with cooking spray; place on grill over medium-hot coals. Place chops on rack, and grill 15 to 20 minutes or to desired degree of doneness, turning and basting frequently with marinade. Yield: 6 servings.

PER SERVING: 159 CALORIES (30% FROM FAT)
FAT 5.3G (SATURATED FAT 1.4G)
PROTEIN 25.1G   CARBOHYDRATE 1.3G
CHOLESTEROL 92MG   SODIUM 118MG

SAVORY ITALIAN-STYLE VEAL CHOPS

4 (6-ounce) lean veal loin chops (¾ inch thick)
¾ teaspoon dried Italian seasoning
⅛ teaspoon pepper
Vegetable cooking spray
¼ cup water
¼ cup dry white wine
½ teaspoon chicken-flavored bouillon granules
1 clove garlic, crushed
1 small onion, thinly sliced
2 cups sliced fresh mushrooms
½ teaspoon dried rosemary, crushed
1 tablespoon chopped fresh parsley

Trim fat from chops; sprinkle chops evenly with Italian seasoning and pepper. Coat a large nonstick skillet with cooking spray; place over medium-high heat until hot. Add chops; cook 3 to 4 minutes on each side or until browned. Remove chops from skillet, and set aside.

Add water and next 3 ingredients to skillet. Bring to a boil; reduce heat, and simmer 2 minutes. Place onion in an 11- x 7- x 1½-inch baking dish coated with cooking spray; top with chops. Pour wine mixture over chops, and top with mushrooms and rosemary. Cover and bake at 350° for 30 to 35 minutes or until chops are tender. Sprinkle chops evenly with parsley. Yield: 4 servings.

PER SERVING: 160 CALORIES (25% FROM FAT)
FAT 4.4G (SATURATED FAT 1.2G)
PROTEIN 24.2G   CARBOHYDRATE 5.4G
CHOLESTEROL 91MG   SODIUM 211MG

Did You Know?

Veal can be as lean as the white meat of chicken. A 3-ounce cooked veal loin chop contains just 149 calories, 90 milligrams of cholesterol, and less than 6 grams of fat.

Fruited Veal Chops Baked in Wine

FRUITED VEAL CHOPS BAKED IN WINE

If you prefer, substitute 1 cup apple juice for the Riesling wine in this recipe.

¼ teaspoon salt
¼ teaspoon pepper
4 (6-ounce) lean veal loin chops (1 inch thick)
Vegetable cooking spray
1 cup chopped onion
1 cup Riesling wine
½ cup canned low-sodium chicken broth, undiluted
¼ cup raisins
1 tablespoon grated orange rind
¼ teaspoon ground sage
¼ teaspoon dried thyme
1 medium Granny Smith apple, peeled and cut into thin wedges
1 medium orange, peeled and sectioned
Fresh sage sprigs (optional)

Sprinkle salt and pepper over chops. Coat a nonstick skillet with cooking spray; place over medium heat until hot. Add chops; cook 2 minutes on each side or until browned. Remove chops from skillet. Drain and pat dry with paper towels.

Place chops in an 11- x 7- x 1½-inch baking dish coated with cooking spray; set aside. Wipe drippings from skillet with a paper towel.

Coat skillet with cooking spray, and place over medium-high heat until hot. Add onion, and sauté until tender. Add wine and next 5 ingredients. Bring to a boil; cover, reduce heat, and simmer 10 minutes. Uncover and simmer 10 minutes.

Arrange apple wedges and orange sections over chops; pour wine mixture over fruit. Bake, uncovered, at 325° for 50 minutes or until chops are tender, basting occasionally with pan juices. To serve, place chops on individual serving plates. Spoon apple mixture over chops. Garnish with sage sprigs, if desired. Yield: 4 servings.

PER SERVING: 196 CALORIES (22% FROM FAT)
FAT 4.7G (SATURATED FAT 1.2G)
PROTEIN 24.0G   CARBOHYDRATE 14.7G
CHOLESTEROL 91MG   SODIUM 266MG

EASY VEAL MILANO

1 pound veal cutlets (¼ inch thick)
3 tablespoons all-purpose flour
¼ teaspoon salt
¼ teaspoon pepper
Vegetable cooking spray
1 teaspoon olive oil
1 cup sliced fresh mushrooms
2 cloves garlic, minced
1 (14½-ounce) can no-salt-added whole tomatoes, undrained and crushed
3 tablespoons sliced ripe olives
¼ teaspoon dried basil
2 cups cooked linguine (cooked without salt or fat)

Trim fat from cutlets; cut cutlets into 2-inch pieces. Combine flour, salt, and pepper; dredge veal in flour mixture.

Coat a nonstick skillet with cooking spray; add oil. Place over medium-high heat until hot. Add veal, and cook 2 minutes on each side or until browned. Remove veal from skillet; set aside, and keep warm.

Coat skillet with cooking spray, and place over medium-high heat until hot. Add mushrooms and garlic; sauté until tender. Stir in tomatoes, olives, and basil; cook over high heat 3 minutes. Return veal to skillet; cover, reduce heat, and simmer 5 minutes. Serve over pasta. Yield: 4 servings.

PER SERVING: 299 CALORIES (19% FROM FAT)
FAT 6.3G (SATURATED FAT 1.4G)
PROTEIN 28.5G   CARBOHYDRATE 31.4G
CHOLESTEROL 94MG   SODIUM 337MG

VEAL SCALOPPINE

1 pound veal cutlets (¼ inch thick)
Freshly ground pepper
Vegetable cooking spray
2 teaspoons olive oil, divided
1 (8-ounce) package fresh mushrooms, sliced
½ small green pepper, cut into thin strips
½ medium-size sweet red pepper, cut into thin strips
½ cup dry white wine
¼ cup canned no-salt-added chicken broth, undiluted
1 tablespoon lemon juice
½ teaspoon salt
1 tablespoon cornstarch
2 tablespoons water
2 tablespoons chopped fresh parsley
2 cups cooked vermicelli (cooked without salt or fat)

Trim fat from cutlets. Place cutlets between 2 sheets of heavy-duty plastic wrap, and flatten to ⅛-inch thickness, using a meat mallet or rolling pin. Sprinkle cutlets with ground pepper.

Coat a large nonstick skillet with cooking spray; add 1 teaspoon oil. Place over medium heat until hot. Add half of veal; cook 3 minutes on each side or until browned. Remove veal from skillet; drain and pat dry with paper towels. Set aside, and keep warm. Wipe drippings from skillet with a paper towel. Repeat procedure with remaining 1 teaspoon oil and half of veal.

Coat skillet with cooking spray, and place over medium heat until hot. Add mushrooms and pepper strips; sauté until crisp-tender. Stir in wine and next 3 ingredients; bring to a boil. Reduce heat; simmer 1 minute.

Combine cornstarch and water, stirring well; add to mushroom mixture. Cook, stirring constantly, until thickened. Remove from heat, and stir in parsley. To serve, place vermicelli on a large serving platter. Arrange veal over vermicelli, and top evenly with sauce. Yield: 4 servings.

PER SERVING: 375 CALORIES (22% FROM FAT)
FAT 9.3G (SATURATED FAT 2.0G)
PROTEIN 34.0G   CARBOHYDRATE 37.5G
CHOLESTEROL 100MG   SODIUM 385MG

VEAL CORDON BLEU

8 veal cutlets (about 1 pound)
½ teaspoon freshly ground pepper
2 (¾-ounce) slices low-fat process Swiss cheese
1 (1-ounce) slice lean cooked ham
2 tablespoons all-purpose flour
¼ cup plus 2 tablespoons frozen egg substitute, thawed
½ cup fine, dry breadcrumbs
Vegetable cooking spray
1 tablespoon reduced-calorie stick margarine
Fresh parsley sprigs (optional)
Lemon slices (optional)

Place cutlets between 2 sheets of wax paper, and flatten to ⅛-inch thickness, using a meat mallet or rolling pin. Sprinkle 4 cutlets with pepper.

Cut each cheese slice in half; place 1 half-slice in center of each of 4 peppered cutlets. Cut ham slice into 4 pieces; place evenly on top of cheese slices. Place remaining 4 cutlets over ham; gently pound edges to seal.

Dredge sealed cutlets in flour, shaking to remove excess flour. Dip cutlets in egg substitute. Dredge in breadcrumbs.

Coat a large nonstick skillet with cooking spray; add margarine. Place over medium-high heat until margarine melts. Add cutlets; cook 2 minutes on each side or until lightly browned. Place cutlets in an 11- x 7- x 1½-inch baking dish coated with cooking spray.

Bake, uncovered, at 375° for 20 minutes. Transfer cutlets to a warm serving platter. If desired, garnish with parsley sprigs and lemon slices. Yield: 4 servings.

PER SERVING: 245 CALORIES (25% FROM FAT)
FAT 6.9G (SATURATED FAT 1.9G)
PROTEIN 31.1G   CARBOHYDRATE 13.1G
CHOLESTEROL 99MG   SODIUM 473MG

VEAL PRIMAVERA

1 pound veal cutlets (¼ inch thick)
2 tablespoons all-purpose flour
Olive oil-flavored vegetable cooking spray
2 teaspoons olive oil
1½ cups sliced fresh mushrooms
1 cup Sugar Snap peas
1 cup julienne-sliced carrot
1 cup julienne-sliced fennel
½ cup canned low-sodium chicken broth,
    undiluted
⅓ cup minced shallots
1 teaspoon dried Italian seasoning
¼ teaspoon salt
¼ teaspoon pepper
1 clove garlic, minced
8 pear-shaped cherry tomatoes, halved
Fresh fennel leaves (optional)

Trim fat from cutlets. Place cutlets between 2 sheets of heavy-duty plastic wrap; flatten to ⅛-inch thickness, using a meat mallet or rolling pin. Sprinkle cutlets evenly with flour.

Coat a large nonstick skillet with cooking spray; add oil. Place over medium-high heat until hot. Add veal, and cook 3 minutes on each side or until done; remove from skillet. Drain and pat dry with paper towels. Set aside, and keep warm. Wipe drippings from skillet with a paper towel.

Add mushrooms and next 9 ingredients to skillet; bring to a boil. Cover, reduce heat, and simmer 2 to 3 minutes or until vegetables are crisp-tender. Add tomatoes, and cook an additional 30 seconds.

To serve, place veal on individual serving plates; spoon vegetable mixture over veal. Garnish with fennel leaves, if desired. Yield: 4 servings.

PER SERVING: 264 CALORIES (30% FROM FAT)
FAT 8.8G (SATURATED FAT 2.0G)
PROTEIN 31.1G   CARBOHYDRATE 15.0G
CHOLESTEROL 100MG   SODIUM 252MG

Veal Primavera

Grilled Honey-Ginger Pork Tenderloins (recipe on page 62)

PASS THE PORK

*Y*es, you really can enjoy pork when following a low-fat eating plan. Leaner cuts of pork are featured in these recipes that range from a fancy crown roast (page 56) to the humble Scrapple (page 69).

The leanest and probably most versatile cut of pork is the tenderloin. It is used in grilled recipes, stir-fries, kabobs, and salads. Turn to page 62 for one of the best recipes, Grilled Honey-Ginger Pork Tenderloins, pictured on the opposite page.

Then the ever-popular pork chop gets special attention on pages 68 and 69. Closing out the chapter are recipes for Honey-Glazed Ham Slices and Hawaiian Ham Kabobs (page 72), along with some helpful information on cooking hams.

Garlic-Ginger Crown Roast of Pork

GARLIC-GINGER CROWN ROAST OF PORK

1 (16-rib) crown roast of pork (about 9
  pounds)
4 large cloves garlic, thinly sliced
1 (1½-inch) piece gingerroot, thinly sliced
2 large cloves garlic, peeled
1 teaspoon vegetable oil
½ teaspoon coarsely ground pepper
Vegetable cooking spray
4 medium-size sweet potatoes, peeled and cut
  into ½-inch slices
2 medium Rome apples, cored and cut into
  ½-inch slices
2 cups unsweetened apple juice, divided
1 tablespoon brown sugar
1 tablespoon lemon juice
½ teaspoon ground ginger, divided
1 tablespoon cornstarch
1 tablespoon water
Fresh watercress sprigs (optional)

Trim fat from roast. Cut ½-inch slits in roast;
place garlic slices and gingerroot slices in slits.

Crush 2 cloves garlic to make a paste. Add oil;
stir well. Brush mixture over roast, and sprinkle
with pepper. Place roast on a rack in a roasting pan
coated with cooking spray. Insert meat thermometer into thickest part of roast, without touching fat
or bone.

Place roast in a 450° oven; reduce heat to 325°,
and bake 2 hours. Drain fat from pan, and arrange
sweet potato and apple around roast.

Combine ¾ cup apple juice, brown sugar, lemon
juice, and ¼ teaspoon ground ginger, stirring well;
pour over sweet potato and apple. Bake an additional 30 minutes or until sweet potato is tender
and meat thermometer registers 160°, basting meat,
sweet potato, and apple frequently with liquid mixture in pan. Remove from oven, and cover loosely
with aluminum foil; let stand 15 minutes.

Combine cornstarch and water in a small saucepan, stirring until smooth. Add remaining 1¼ cups apple juice and ¼ teaspoon ground ginger, stirring well. Bring to a boil; cook, stirring constantly, 1 minute or until thickened.

Transfer roast to a serving platter. Arrange sweet potato and apple around roast; drizzle with juice mixture. Garnish with fresh watercress sprigs, if desired. Serve remaining apple juice mixture with roast. Yield: 16 servings.

PER SERVING: 278 CALORIES (30% FROM FAT)
FAT 9.4G (SATURATED FAT 3.1G)
PROTEIN 27.5G CARBOHYDRATE 20.3G
CHOLESTEROL 81MG   SODIUM 72MG

PORK ROAST WITH CHERRY SAUCE

Expecting company? Keep the menu simple by serving this roast with commercial wild rice pilaf and steamed broccoli.

1 (2½-pound) lean boneless double pork loin roast, tied
½ teaspoon ground ginger
½ teaspoon dry mustard
½ teaspoon pepper
Vegetable cooking spray
2 tablespoons honey
2 tablespoons fine, dry breadcrumbs
1 cup dry white wine
1 tablespoon balsamic vinegar
½ cup unsweetened pitted dried cherries
¼ cup firmly packed brown sugar
2 teaspoons cornstarch
1 tablespoon water

Untie roast, and trim fat. Retie roast. Combine ginger, dry mustard, and pepper; rub mixture over surface of roast. Place roast on a rack in a roasting pan coated with cooking spray. Insert meat thermometer into thickest part of roast. Place roast in a 450° oven. Reduce heat to 350°, and bake 1 hour and 15 minutes.

Brush roast with honey, and sprinkle with breadcrumbs. Combine wine and vinegar; pour over roast. Bake, uncovered, an additional 30 minutes or until meat thermometer registers 160°.

Remove roast from pan, reserving drippings. Let roast stand 10 minutes. Skim fat from drippings, and place drippings in a small saucepan. Bring to a boil; add cherries, and simmer 10 minutes.

Combine brown sugar, cornstarch, and water; stir well. Add to cherry mixture. Cook, stirring constantly, until thickened.

Remove string from roast; cut diagonally across grain into ¼-inch-thick slices. Serve with cherry sauce. Yield: 10 servings.

Note: Raisins may be substituted for dried cherries, if desired.

PER SERVING: 235 CALORIES (31% FROM FAT)
FAT 8.2G (SATURATED FAT 2.8G)
PROTEIN 21.8G CARBOHYDRATE 18.4G
CHOLESTEROL 61MG   SODIUM 80MG

When the recipe calls for a double pork loin roast, first trim any fat on the outside of the roast. Then open up the roast, and trim the fat on the inside. Retie the roast at 2- to 3-inch intervals with heavy string before cooking.

Colorful Stuffed Pork Roast

COLORFUL STUFFED PORK ROAST

2 (6-ounce) packages long-grain and wild rice
   mix
¾ cup boiling water
¾ cup dried apricots
Vegetable cooking spray
¾ cup chopped fresh mushrooms
½ cup chopped green onions
½ cup chopped sweet red pepper
2 cloves garlic, minced
¼ cup plus 2 tablespoons chopped water
   chestnuts
2 tablespoons chopped fresh parsley
½ teaspoon freshly ground pepper
1 (4-pound) lean boneless double pork loin
   roast, tied
½ cup apricot jam, melted and divided

Prepare rice mix according to package directions, omitting salt and fat. Set aside.

Pour boiling water over apricots; let stand 20 minutes. Drain well. Finely chop apricots, and set aside.

Coat a large nonstick skillet with cooking spray; place over medium-high heat until hot. Add mushrooms, green onions, sweet red pepper, and garlic; sauté 4 to 5 minutes or until vegetables are tender. Stir in rice, apricots, water chestnuts, parsley, and ground pepper.

Untie roast, and trim fat. Spread 1¼ cups rice mixture over inside of roast. Retie roast. Set remaining rice mixture aside; keep warm. Place roast on a rack in a roasting pan coated with cooking spray; brush roast with half of jam. Insert meat thermometer into thickest part of roast. Bake at 350° for 1 hour and 40 minutes or until meat thermometer registers 160°, basting frequently with remaining half of jam.

Let roast stand 10 minutes. Spread remaining rice mixture on a large serving platter; place roast on top of rice mixture. Remove string from roast; slice diagonally across grain into 16 slices. Yield: 16 servings.

PER SERVING: 309 CALORIES (31% FROM FAT)
FAT 10.7G (SATURATED FAT 3.7G)
PROTEIN 22.8G   CARBOHYDRATE 30.2G
CHOLESTEROL 67MG   SODIUM 418MG

PORK ROAST WITH BRAISED VEGETABLES

1 (2½-pound) rolled boneless pork loin roast
1 tablespoon chopped fresh rosemary, divided
1 tablespoon chopped fresh thyme, divided
1 teaspoon salt, divided
¼ teaspoon pepper, divided
Vegetable cooking spray
12 unpeeled small round red potatoes, halved
8 large shallots, peeled
8 ripe plum tomatoes, quartered
6 cloves garlic
1 (9-ounce) package frozen artichoke hearts, thawed
¾ cup canned low-sodium chicken broth, undiluted
¼ cup fresh lemon juice
1½ teaspoons olive oil

Unroll roast, and trim fat. Combine 1 teaspoon rosemary, 1 teaspoon thyme, and ¼ teaspoon salt; rub inside surface of roast with rosemary mixture. Reroll roast; secure at 1-inch intervals with heavy string. Combine 1 teaspoon rosemary, 1 teaspoon thyme, ¼ teaspoon salt, and ⅛ teaspoon pepper; sprinkle over roast.

Coat a large Dutch oven with cooking spray; place over medium-high heat until hot. Add roast, and cook until browned on all sides; remove pan from heat. Insert meat thermometer into thickest part of roast.

Arrange potato and next 4 ingredients around

roast. Pour broth, lemon juice, and oil over vegetables, and sprinkle with remaining 1 teaspoon rosemary, 1 teaspoon thyme, ½ teaspoon salt, and ⅛ teaspoon pepper. Cover and bake at 425° for 20 minutes; reduce heat to 325°, and bake 1 hour or until meat thermometer registers 160°.

Place roast on a platter. Drain vegetables, reserving 1¾ cups cooking liquid. Reserve 8 potato halves; arrange remaining vegetables around roast.

Combine reserved cooking liquid and 8 potato halves in container of an electric blender; cover and process until smooth. Serve potato gravy with pork and vegetables. Yield: 8 servings.

PER SERVING: 339 CALORIES (28% FROM FAT)
FAT 10.4G (SATURATED FAT 3.3G)
PROTEIN 29.6G   CARBOHYDRATE 33.2G
CHOLESTEROL 70MG   SODIUM 410MG

PORK TENDERLOINS WITH SAGE-CRUMB COATING

2 (½-pound) pork tenderloins
Vegetable cooking spray
1½ tablespoons Dijon mustard
1 cup soft whole wheat breadcrumbs
2 teaspoons rubbed sage
⅛ teaspoon pepper
1 clove garlic, minced

Trim fat from tenderloins; place tenderloins on a rack in a shallow roasting pan coated with cooking spray. Brush tenderloins evenly with mustard.

Combine breadcrumbs and remaining ingredients; rub mixture over tenderloins.

Insert meat thermometer into thickest part of one tenderloin. Bake at 400° for 30 to 35 minutes or until meat thermometer registers 160°. Yield: 4 servings.

PER SERVING: 159 CALORIES (21% FROM FAT)
FAT 3.7G (SATURATED FAT 1.0G)
PROTEIN 24.8G   CARBOHYDRATE 5.1G
CHOLESTEROL 74MG   SODIUM 270MG

Orange-Glazed Pork

ORANGE-GLAZED PORK

1½ pounds pork tenderloin
Vegetable cooking spray
1 cup water
¼ cup honey
1½ teaspoons ground cinnamon
2 teaspoons peeled, grated gingerroot
1 teaspoon grated orange rind
¼ teaspoon salt
⅛ teaspoon pepper
1 teaspoon cornstarch
¼ cup unsweetened orange juice
1 cup orange sections (about 3 oranges)
Orange leaves (optional)

Trim fat from pork; place pork on a rack in a shallow roasting pan coated with cooking spray. Pour 1 cup water into roasting pan. Combine honey and next 5 ingredients in a small bowl, and brush over pork. Insert a meat thermometer into the thickest part of pork.

Bake at 400° for 30 minutes or until meat thermometer registers 160°. Remove pork from rack; set aside, and keep warm. Skim fat from pan drippings.

Place cornstarch and orange juice in a small saucepan, stirring with a wire whisk until blended. Pour roasting pan drippings into pan; bring to a boil, and cook 1 minute. Remove from heat, and gently stir in orange sections. Cut pork into ½-inch-thick slices. Serve with orange sauce. Garnish with orange leaves, if desired. Yield: 6 servings.

PER SERVING: 193 CALORIES (14% FROM FAT)
FAT 3.0G (SATURATED FAT 1.0G)
PROTEIN 24.2G CARBOHYDRATE 17.3G
CHOLESTEROL 74MG SODIUM 154MG

SPICED PORK BARBECUE

1 (2-pound) boneless pork sirloin roast
Vegetable cooking spray
2 (14½-ounce) cans no-salt-added whole
    tomatoes, undrained and chopped
1⅓ cups chopped onion
⅓ cup raisins
2 tablespoons no-salt-added tomato paste
2 tablespoons cider vinegar
1 tablespoon minced pickled jalapeño slices
1 teaspoon beef-flavored bouillon granules
¼ teaspoon salt
¼ teaspoon ground cinnamon
⅛ teaspoon ground cloves

Trim fat from roast. Cut roast into 2-inch pieces. Coat a Dutch oven with cooking spray; place over medium heat until hot. Add pork; cook until browned on all sides. Drain; pat dry with paper towels. Wipe drippings from pan with a paper towel.

Return pork to pan; add tomato and remaining ingredients, stirring well. Bring to a boil; cover, reduce heat, and simmer 1½ hours or until pork is very tender. Uncover and cook over medium-high heat 8 minutes or until liquid evaporates, stirring often. Remove from heat; let cool slightly. Shred pork using two forks. Return pork to pan; cook until heated. Yield: 8 servings.

PER SERVING: 216 CALORIES (32% FROM FAT)
FAT 7.6G (SATURATED FAT 0.8G)
PROTEIN 24.2G CARBOHYDRATE 12.5G
CHOLESTEROL 68MG SODIUM 291MG

Health Tip

Recent scientific research has shown that low blood levels of HDL cholesterol ("good" cholesterol) may be a significant danger sign for heart disease. How do you raise your HDL? Exercise! And if you are overweight, try to lose a few pounds.

GRILLED HONEY-GINGER PORK TENDERLOINS

(pictured on page 54)

For an even richer flavor, let the pork tenderloins marinate in the refrigerator for 8 hours or overnight.

2 (½-pound) pork tenderloins
¼ cup plus 2 tablespoons low-sodium soy
    sauce
1 tablespoon peeled, minced gingerroot
1 tablespoon minced garlic
3 tablespoons honey
1 tablespoon reduced-calorie ketchup
¼ teaspoon onion powder
¼ teaspoon ground red pepper
¼ teaspoon ground cinnamon
Vegetable cooking spray
Fresh flat-leaf parsley sprigs (optional)

Place pork in an 11- x 7- x 1½-inch baking dish. Combine soy sauce and next 7 ingredients, stirring well; pour over pork. Cover and marinate in refrigerator at least 15 minutes, turning once.

Remove pork from marinade, reserving marinade. Coat grill rack with cooking spray; place on grill over medium-hot coals. Place pork on rack, and insert meat thermometer into thickest part of pork. Grill 20 to 25 minutes or until meat thermometer registers 160°, turning frequently. Let pork stand 10 minutes. Slice diagonally across grain into thin slices, and transfer to a serving platter.

Place reserved marinade in a saucepan; bring to a boil. Reduce heat, and simmer 3 minutes. Spoon mixture evenly over pork. Garnish with fresh parsley sprigs, if desired. Yield: 4 servings.

PER SERVING: 219 CALORIES (19% FROM FAT)
FAT 4.6G (SATURATED FAT 1.5G)
PROTEIN 26.8G   CARBOHYDRATE 14.6G
CHOLESTEROL 86MG   SODIUM 648MG

CURRIED PORK MEDAILLONS

2 (¾-pound) pork tenderloins
2 teaspoons reduced-calorie margarine
2 medium-size firm bananas, peeled and cut
    into ½-inch-thick slices
½ teaspoon ground cinnamon
Vegetable cooking spray
1¼ cups unsweetened orange juice, divided
¾ cup thinly sliced green onions
1 medium-size sweet red pepper, cut into thin
    strips
1½ teaspoons cornstarch
¼ cup plus 2 tablespoons raisins
1 teaspoon curry powder
½ teaspoon ground cumin

Trim fat from tenderloins, and cut diagonally across grain into ¼-inch-thick slices; set aside.

Melt margarine in a large nonstick skillet over medium-high heat. Add banana and cinnamon; sauté 5 minutes or until golden, tossing gently. Transfer to a bowl, and keep warm.

Coat skillet with cooking spray, and place over medium-high heat until hot. Add half of pork, and cook 3 minutes on each side or until pork is lightly browned. Remove pork from skillet, and drain. Repeat procedure with remaining pork. Wipe drippings from skillet with a paper towel.

Combine 2 tablespoons orange juice, green onions, and red pepper in skillet; stir well. Cook over medium-high heat, stirring constantly, 2 minutes or until vegetables are tender.

Combine cornstarch and remaining 1 cup plus 2 tablespoons orange juice, stirring until smooth. Add cornstarch mixture to vegetable mixture in skillet; stir well. Add raisins, curry powder, and cumin. Bring to a boil; reduce heat, and simmer, stirring constantly, 1 minute. Return pork to skillet, and simmer an additional 3 to 4 minutes or until pork is tender, stirring often. Serve with banana slices. Yield: 6 servings.

PER SERVING: 258 CALORIES (20% FROM FAT)
FAT 5.7G (SATURATED FAT 1.7G)
PROTEIN 27.4G   CARBOHYDRATE 25.2G
CHOLESTEROL 83MG   SODIUM 78MG

PORK MEDAILLONS WITH ARTICHOKE SAUCE

1 (9-ounce) package frozen artichoke hearts
1 cup canned no-salt-added chicken broth, undiluted
2 (¾-pound) pork tenderloins
Olive oil-flavored vegetable cooking spray
1 teaspoon olive oil
1 cup sliced fresh mushrooms
2 tablespoons chopped shallots
2½ tablespoons all-purpose flour
1½ cups skim milk
¼ cup grated Asiago cheese
¼ teaspoon salt
¼ teaspoon pepper
¼ teaspoon dry mustard

Cook artichoke hearts in chicken broth according to package directions, omitting salt; drain well. Coarsely chop artichoke hearts, and set aside.

Trim fat from tenderloins, and cut pork into ½-inch-thick slices. Coat a large nonstick skillet with cooking spray, and place over medium-high heat until hot. Add pork slices, and cook until browned on both sides, turning once. Drain and pat dry with paper towels. Wipe drippings from skillet with a paper towel. Set pork aside.

Coat skillet with cooking spray; add oil. Place over medium-high heat until hot. Add mushrooms and shallots; sauté until tender. Remove mushroom mixture from skillet, and set aside. Wipe drippings from skillet with a paper towel.

Combine flour and milk in skillet, stirring with a wire whisk until smooth. Cook over medium heat, stirring constantly, until thickened. Stir in chopped artichoke, mushroom mixture, cheese, and remaining ingredients; add pork. Cover and cook over medium heat 10 minutes or until pork is tender. Yield: 6 servings.

PER SERVING: 226 CALORIES (26% FROM FAT)
FAT 6.5G (SATURATED FAT 2.5G)
PROTEIN 30.9G CARBOHYDRATE 10.2G
CHOLESTEROL 87MG SODIUM 267MG

PORK MEDAILLONS WITH SWEET PEPPERS
(pictured on page 2)

¼ cup all-purpose flour
¼ teaspoon dried basil
⅛ teaspoon salt
⅛ teaspoon pepper
1 pound pork tenderloin
Vegetable cooking spray
1 teaspoon vegetable oil
1 small sweet red pepper, seeded and cut into very thin strips
1 small sweet yellow pepper, seeded and cut into very thin strips
1 small green pepper, seeded and cut into very thin strips
2 teaspoons minced shallots
3 tablespoons dry white vermouth
3 tablespoons water
1 teaspoon cornstarch
½ teaspoon dried sage
¼ teaspoon chicken-flavored bouillon granules

Combine first 4 ingredients in a small bowl; stir well. Cut pork into ½-inch-thick slices; dredge pork medaillons in flour mixture.

Coat a large nonstick skillet with cooking spray; add oil. Place over medium-high heat until hot. Add pork slices; cook 4 to 5 minutes on each side or until done. Remove pork from skillet. Drain and pat dry with paper towels; set pork aside, and keep warm. Wipe drippings from skillet with a paper towel.

Coat skillet with cooking spray, and place over medium-high heat until hot. Add peppers and shallots; sauté 5 to 7 minutes or until peppers are crisp-tender.

Combine vermouth and remaining ingredients, stirring well; add to skillet. Bring to a boil; reduce heat, and cook, stirring constantly, until thickened. Spoon pepper mixture onto a large serving platter; arrange pork over peppers. Yield: 4 servings.

PER SERVING: 217 CALORIES (26% FROM FAT)
FAT 6.3G (SATURATED FAT 1.8G)
PROTEIN 27.3G CARBOHYDRATE 11.6G
CHOLESTEROL 83MG SODIUM 218MG

Pork-and-Vegetable Piccata

PORK-AND-VEGETABLE PICCATA

Flat-leaf, or Italian, parsley has a stronger flavor than the more common curly-leaf parsley and is preferred for this recipe.

1 pound pork tenderloin
Vegetable cooking spray
1 teaspoon olive oil
3 cups small fresh broccoli flowerets
3 cups sliced yellow squash
¼ cup chopped flat-leaf or curly-leaf parsley
½ teaspoon ground white pepper
¼ teaspoon salt
2 cloves garlic, crushed
¼ cup fresh lemon juice, divided
¾ cup canned low-sodium chicken broth,
    undiluted
¼ cup extra-dry vermouth
1 teaspoon grated lemon rind
2 cloves garlic, crushed
1 tablespoon drained capers
½ teaspoon paprika

Trim fat from pork, and cut crosswise into 16 pieces. Place each piece between 2 sheets of heavy-duty plastic wrap, and flatten to ¼-inch thickness, using a meat mallet or rolling pin. Set pork aside.

Coat a large nonstick skillet with cooking spray; add oil, and place over medium-high heat until hot. Add broccoli and next 5 ingredients; sauté 6 minutes or until crisp-tender. Remove from heat. Add 2 tablespoons lemon juice; toss well. Spoon vegetable mixture onto a serving platter; set aside, and keep warm.

Recoat skillet with cooking spray; place over medium-high heat until hot. Add one-third of pork; cook 2 minutes on each side or until done. Repeat procedure with remaining pork. Drain pork on paper towels; place pork on serving platter with vegetable mixture, and keep warm. Wipe drippings from skillet with a paper towel.

Add broth and next 3 ingredients to skillet; scrape bottom of skillet with a wooden spoon to loosen browned bits. Bring to a boil; cook 2½

minutes. Remove from heat; stir in remaining 2 tablespoons lemon juice, capers, and paprika. Spoon over vegetables and pork. Yield: 4 servings.

PER SERVING: 199 CALORIES (23% FROM FAT)
FAT 5.1G (SATURATED FAT 1.2G)
PROTEIN 27.9G   CARBOHYDRATE 11.8G
CHOLESTEROL 74MG   SODIUM 408MG

SESAME PORK BROCHETTES

1½ pounds lean boneless pork loin (½ inch
     thick)
¼ cup honey
2 tablespoons sesame seeds, toasted and divided
3 tablespoons lemon juice
1 tablespoon low-sodium soy sauce
¾ teaspoon ground cumin
½ teaspoon ground cinnamon
Vegetable cooking spray
3 cups cooked couscous (cooked without salt
    or fat)

Trim fat from pork; cut pork into ¼-inch-wide strips. Place pork in a large shallow dish.

Combine honey, 1 tablespoon plus 1 teaspoon sesame seeds, lemon juice, soy sauce, cumin, and cinnamon in container of an electric blender; cover and process until smooth. Pour over pork. Cover and marinate in refrigerator 2 hours.

Remove pork from marinade, reserving marinade. Thread pork onto 12 (10-inch) skewers. Place skewers on rack of a broiler pan coated with cooking spray. Broil 5½ inches from heat (with electric oven door partially opened) 4 minutes. Turn and baste with reserved marinade; broil an additional 4 minutes or until done.

To serve, place couscous on a large serving platter. Arrange skewers over couscous, and sprinkle evenly with remaining 2 teaspoons toasted sesame seeds. Serve immediately. Yield: 6 servings.

PER SERVING: 357 CALORIES (26% FROM FAT)
FAT 10.4G (SATURATED FAT 3.3G)
PROTEIN 31.4G   CARBOHYDRATE 33.4G
CHOLESTEROL 83MG   SODIUM 134MG

MARINATED PORK-AND-VEGETABLE KABOBS

12 small unpeeled round red potatoes (about 1
    pound)
12 large fresh mushrooms
1   pound pork tenderloin
16 (½-inch) slices zucchini
1   large green pepper, cut into 24 (1-inch)
    pieces
1   large sweet red pepper, cut into 24 (1-inch)
    pieces
½   cup canned low-sodium chicken broth,
    undiluted
1   tablespoon chopped fresh oregano
1   tablespoon chopped fresh thyme
2   tablespoons lemon juice
1   tablespoon olive oil
½   teaspoon salt
½   teaspoon pepper
3   cloves garlic, crushed
Vegetable cooking spray

Place potatoes in a saucepan, and add water to
cover. Bring to a boil, and cook 15 minutes or until
tender; drain. Pour cold water over potatoes; drain.
Cut potatoes in half, and set aside.

Discard mushroom stems, and halve mushroom
caps lengthwise; set aside.

Trim fat from pork, and cut pork into 16 (1½-
inch) cubes. Combine pork, potatoes, mushrooms,
zucchini, and green and red peppers in a large
heavy-duty, zip-top plastic bag. Add chicken broth
and next 7 ingredients; seal bag, and marinate in
refrigerator for 2 hours, turning bag occasionally.

Remove pork and vegetables from bag. Place
marinade in a saucepan, and bring to a boil; set
aside.

Thread 3 potato halves, 3 mushroom halves, 2
pork cubes, 2 zucchini slices, 3 green pepper
pieces, and 3 red pepper pieces alternately onto
each of 8 (12-inch) skewers.

Marinated Pork-and-Vegetable Kabobs

Coat grill rack with cooking spray; place rack on grill over medium-hot coals. Place kabobs on grill rack, and grill 6 minutes on each side or until pork is done, basting occasionally with the reserved marinade. Yield: 4 servings.

PER SERVING: 305 CALORIES (25% FROM FAT)
FAT 8.6G (SATURATED FAT 2.1G)
PROTEIN 29.8G CARBOHYDRATE 28.6G
CHOLESTEROL 79MG SODIUM 374MG

PORK WITH BABY CORN

½ pound lean boneless pork loin
1 cup diced sweet red pepper
1 tablespoon low-sodium soy sauce
1 tablespoon dry sherry
1 teaspoon sugar
⅔ cup water
1 tablespoon cornstarch
2 tablespoons low-sodium soy sauce
1 to 2 teaspoons chili puree with garlic sauce
Vegetable cooking spray
2 teaspoons vegetable oil
1 (15-ounce) can whole baby corn, drained
1 (8-ounce) can sliced water chestnuts, drained
1 (4½-ounce) jar sliced mushrooms, drained
2 teaspoons dark sesame oil
4 cups cooked long-grain rice (cooked without salt or fat)

Trim fat from pork, and cut pork into thin strips. Combine pork and next 4 ingredients in a bowl; stir well, and set aside. Combine water and next 3 ingredients; stir well, and set aside.

Coat a large nonstick skillet with cooking spray; add oil, and place over medium heat until hot. Add pork mixture; sauté 2 minutes. Add corn, water chestnuts, and mushrooms; sauté 3 minutes. Add cornstarch mixture; bring to a boil, and cook 1 minute or until thickened. Remove from heat; drizzle sesame oil over the pork mixture. Serve over rice. Yield: 4 servings.

PER SERVING: 405 CALORIES (22% FROM FAT)
FAT 9.7G (SATURATED FAT 2.4G)
PROTEIN 18.4G CARBOHYDRATE 57.8G
CHOLESTEROL 34MG SODIUM 674MG

PORK WITH BROCCOLI-MUSHROOM STIR-FRY

2 tablespoons cornstarch
1 teaspoon sugar
1 teaspoon dried crushed red pepper
½ teaspoon salt
⅔ cup canned low-sodium chicken broth, undiluted
¼ cup rice vinegar
¼ cup low-sodium soy sauce
2 teaspoons dark sesame oil
1 pound pork tenderloin
1 tablespoon cornstarch
2 teaspoons vegetable oil
Vegetable cooking spray
2 teaspoons peeled, grated gingerroot
2 cloves garlic, minced
4 cups fresh broccoli flowerets
3 cups sliced fresh mushrooms
1 tablespoon sesame seeds
1½ cups sliced green onions
6 cups cooked long-grain rice (cooked without salt or fat)

Combine first 8 ingredients in a bowl; stir well, and set aside. Trim fat from pork, and cut pork in half lengthwise. Cut each half crosswise into thin slices. Combine pork, 1 tablespoon cornstarch, and vegetable oil in a bowl; toss well.

Coat a large nonstick skillet with cooking spray; place over medium-high heat until hot. Add pork mixture; stir-fry 4 minutes or until browned. Remove pork from skillet; set aside.

Add gingerroot and garlic to skillet; stir-fry 30 seconds. Add broccoli; stir-fry 2 minutes. Add mushrooms and sesame seeds; stir-fry 2 minutes. Return pork to skillet. Add green onions and broth mixture; bring to a boil. Cook, stirring constantly, 1 minute or until thickened. Serve over rice. Yield: 6 servings.

PER SERVING: 408 CALORIES (15% FROM FAT)
FAT 6.6G (SATURATED FAT 1.3G)
PROTEIN 24.0G CARBOHYDRATE 63.0G
CHOLESTEROL 49MG SODIUM 586MG

CRANBERRY-GINGER PORK CHOPS

4 (6-ounce) lean center-cut pork loin chops
½ cup cranberry juice cocktail concentrate,
    thawed and undiluted
3 tablespoons sliced green onions
1 tablespoon peeled, grated gingerroot
¼ teaspoon ground red pepper
Vegetable cooking spray

Trim fat from chops. Place chops in a heavy-duty, zip-top plastic bag. Combine cranberry juice cocktail concentrate and next 3 ingredients; pour over chops. Seal bag; shake until chops are well coated. Marinate in refrigerator 8 hours, turning bag occasionally.

Remove chops from marinade. Place marinade in a saucepan, and bring to a boil; set aside.

Coat grill rack with cooking spray, and place on grill over medium-hot coals. Place chops on rack, and grill 5 to 6 minutes on each side or until desired degree of doneness, basting frequently with marinade. Yield: 4 servings.

PER SERVING: 342 CALORIES (30% FROM FAT)
FAT 11.4G (SATURATED FAT 4.1G)
PROTEIN 24.4G CARBOHYDRATE 34.7G
CHOLESTEROL 77MG SODIUM 69MG

Trim any fat around the edge of bone-in or boneless pork chops to keep them as low in fat as possible.

PORK CHOPS WITH POTATO STUFFING

2 cups diced unpeeled round red potato
6 (5-ounce) lean center-cut pork loin chops
    (½ inch thick)
Vegetable cooking spray
¾ cup skim milk
⅓ cup canned no-salt-added chicken broth,
    undiluted
1 teaspoon lemon juice
¼ teaspoon pepper
2 tablespoons all-purpose flour
1 teaspoon vegetable oil
⅓ cup chopped green onions
¼ cup diced celery
1 clove garlic, minced
1½ cups herb-seasoned stuffing mix
½ teaspoon rubbed sage
1 cup water

Cook potato in boiling water 10 minutes or until tender; drain and set aside.

Trim fat from chops. Coat a nonstick skillet with cooking spray; place over medium-high heat until hot. Add chops; cook 2½ minutes on each side. Remove from skillet; drain and set aside.

Wipe drippings from pan with a paper towel; return chops to skillet. Add milk, broth, lemon juice, and pepper; bring to a boil. Cover, reduce heat, and simmer 30 minutes or until chops are tender. Remove 3 tablespoons cooking liquid; let cool. Combine flour and reserved cooking liquid; stir well. Add to skillet; cook until thickened and bubbly. Set aside, and keep warm.

Coat a large skillet with cooking spray; add oil, and place over medium-high heat until hot. Add green onions, celery, and garlic; sauté 3 minutes or until tender. Add potato; sauté 5 minutes or until browned. Add stuffing mix, sage, and water; stir well. Reduce heat; cover and cook 3 minutes.

To serve, top each chop with ½ cup stuffing mixture. Serve with gravy. Yield: 6 servings.

PER SERVING: 300 CALORIES (32% FROM FAT)
FAT 10.7G (SATURATED FAT 3.4G)
PROTEIN 22.1G CARBOHYDRATE 28.0G
CHOLESTEROL 60MG SODIUM 355MG

PORK CHOPS WITH APPLES AND SWEET POTATOES

2 teaspoons vegetable oil
5 (5-ounce) lean center-cut pork loin chops (about ½ inch thick)
2½ cups (½-inch) cubed peeled sweet potato (about 1 pound)
½ cup thinly sliced onion
1¾ cups unsweetened orange juice, divided
⅓ cup firmly packed dark brown sugar
2 tablespoons cider vinegar
¼ teaspoon salt
2 tablespoons cornstarch
2½ cups (½-inch) cubed Rome apple (about ¾ pound)

Heat oil in a large nonstick skillet over medium-high heat. Add pork chops; cook 3 minutes on each side or until browned. Remove from skillet, and drain on paper towels; set pork chops aside, and keep warm.

Add sweet potato and sliced onion to skillet, and sauté 3 minutes or until tender. Combine 1½ cups orange juice and next 3 ingredients, and stir well. Return chops to skillet; pour orange juice mixture over chops. Cover, reduce heat, and simmer 1 hour or until chops are tender.

Remove pork chops from skillet; set aside, and keep warm. Combine remaining ¼ cup orange juice and cornstarch; stir well, and add to skillet. Stir in apple; bring to a boil over medium heat, and cook, stirring constantly, 1 minute. Serve over pork chops. Yield: 5 servings.

PER SERVING: 410 CALORIES (23% FROM FAT)
FAT 10.3G (SATURATED FAT 3.2G)
PROTEIN 26.8G CARBOHYDRATE 52.5G
CHOLESTEROL 72MG SODIUM 207MG

SCRAPPLE

This classic sausage loaf is traditionally made with scraps of cooked pork (hence its name) and cornmeal mush. We've used lean pork to keep the fat low.

1 (1-pound) lean boneless pork roast
1 medium onion, quartered
½ teaspoon black peppercorns
1 bay leaf
8 cups water
3 green onions, coarsely chopped
¾ teaspoon dried sage
½ teaspoon dried thyme
½ teaspoon pepper
1½ cups white cornmeal
¾ cup cold water
¾ teaspoon salt
Vegetable cooking spray

Combine first 5 ingredients in a large Dutch oven, and bring to a boil. Cover, reduce heat, and simmer 1½ hours or until pork is tender. Remove pork from broth, and let cool. Strain broth, reserving 4 cups. Discard onion, peppercorns, and bay leaf. Cover and chill reserved broth 8 hours.

Place pork, green onions, sage, thyme, and pepper in food processor bowl, and process 15 seconds or until pork is finely chopped. Cover and chill.

Combine cornmeal and ¾ cup cold water, and let stand 5 minutes. Skim and discard fat from reserved broth; bring broth to a boil in Dutch oven. Add cornmeal mixture and salt; bring to a boil, and cook, stirring constantly, 2 minutes. Cover, reduce heat, and simmer 20 minutes, stirring occasionally.

Remove cornmeal mixture from heat; add pork mixture, stirring well. Spoon mixture into 3 (5- x 2½- x 2-inch) loafpans that have been lined with heavy-duty plastic wrap. Cover; chill at least 3 hours or until set. Unmold; cut into ½-inch slices.

Coat a large nonstick skillet with cooking spray, and place over medium-high heat until hot. Add slices of pork mixture, and cook 5 minutes on each side or until browned. Yield: 6 servings.

PER SERVING: 267 CALORIES (29% FROM FAT)
FAT 8.5G (SATURATED FAT 2.8G)
PROTEIN 18.2G CARBOHYDRATE 27.6G
CHOLESTEROL 51MG SODIUM 334MG

PORK-FILLED CABBAGE LEAVES

2 quarts water
8 large cabbage leaves
1 pound lean ground pork
1 cup cooked long-grain rice (cooked without
    salt or fat)
½ cup minced onion
¼ cup finely chopped green pepper
1 egg, lightly beaten
½ teaspoon dried thyme
¼ teaspoon salt
¼ teaspoon pepper
Vegetable cooking spray
1 (14½-ounce) can no-salt-added stewed
    tomatoes, undrained
½ cup canned no-salt-added beef broth,
    undiluted
1 tablespoon brown sugar
2 tablespoons lemon juice

Bring water to a boil in a large saucepan. Add cabbage leaves to water, one at a time. Cover, reduce heat, and simmer 4 minutes. Drain and rinse under cold water; drain again. Cut a small V-shape in the base of each leaf to remove thick center core; discard cores.

Combine pork and next 7 ingredients. Spoon pork mixture evenly in centers of cabbage leaves; fold ends over, and roll up.

Coat a large nonstick skillet with cooking spray. Place cabbage rolls in skillet, seam side down. Combine tomatoes, broth, brown sugar, and lemon juice; pour over cabbage rolls. Bring to a boil; cover, reduce heat, and simmer 1 hour. Serve warm. Yield: 8 servings.

PER SERVING: 164 CALORIES (28% FROM FAT)
FAT 5.1G (SATURATED FAT 1.7G)
PROTEIN 14.3G CARBOHYDRATE 15.0G
CHOLESTEROL 62MG SODIUM 137MG

GRILLED TENDERLOIN SALAD

2 tablespoons honey
1 tablespoon Dijon mustard
¼ teaspoon ground ginger
2 (½-pound) pork tenderloins
Vegetable cooking spray
⅓ cup plus 1 tablespoon nonfat mayonnaise-
    type salad dressing
⅓ cup plus 1 tablespoon unsweetened
    pineapple juice
2 tablespoons honey
1 tablespoon Dijon mustard
¼ teaspoon ground ginger
2 cups tightly packed torn leaf lettuce
2 cups tightly packed torn curly endive
2 cups cubed fresh pineapple
¼ cup thinly sliced purple onion, separated
    into rings
12 (½-inch-thick) slices peeled cantaloupe
¼ cup sliced almonds, toasted

Combine first 3 ingredients in a small bowl. Trim fat from pork; brush honey mixture over pork.

Coat grill rack with cooking spray, and place on grill over medium-hot coals. Place pork on rack, and insert meat thermometer into thickest part of 1 tenderloin. Grill 18 minutes or until meat thermometer registers 160°, turning pork occasionally. Cut pork into ¼-inch-thick slices; set aside.

Combine salad dressing and next 4 ingredients in container of an electric blender; cover and process until smooth. To serve, divide pork, lettuces, pineapple, onion, and cantaloupe evenly among 6 serving plates. Top each salad with 2 teaspoons almonds. Serve each with 2½ tablespoons dressing. Yield: 6 servings.

PER SERVING: 250 CALORIES (21% FROM FAT)
FAT 5.7G (SATURATED FAT 1.3G)
PROTEIN 18.4G CARBOHYDRATE 32.9G
CHOLESTEROL 53MG SODIUM 420MG

Grecian Pork Tenderloin Salad

GRECIAN PORK TENDERLOIN SALAD

1 pound pork tenderloin
1 teaspoon chopped fresh oregano
1½ tablespoons red wine vinegar
1½ teaspoons olive oil
1 clove garlic, crushed
1½ cups peeled, sliced cucumber, divided
1 tablespoon coarsely chopped fresh dill
1 (8-ounce) carton plain nonfat yogurt
4 cups tightly packed torn romaine lettuce
½ cup thinly sliced onion, separated into rings
½ cup thinly sliced radishes
2 tablespoons crumbled feta cheese
2 teaspoons chopped fresh mint
2 medium unpeeled ripe tomatoes, each cut
     into 8 wedges
1 medium-size green pepper, sliced crosswise
8 pitted, whole ripe olives

Trim fat from pork. Combine oregano, vinegar, oil, and garlic in a large heavy-duty, zip-top plastic bag. Add pork; seal bag, and marinate in refrigerator 30 minutes, turning bag occasionally.

Position knife blade in food processor bowl; add ½ cup cucumber, dill, and yogurt. Process 10 seconds or until smooth; set aside.

Remove pork from bag. Place marinade in a saucepan, and bring to a boil; set aside.

Place pork on grill rack over medium-hot coals. Insert meat thermometer into thickest part of pork. Cover; grill 30 minutes or until thermometer registers 160°, turning pork occasionally and basting with reserved marinade. Thinly slice pork, and set aside.

To serve, divide lettuce among 4 plates; top with remaining cucumber, onion, and remaining ingredients. Divide pork among plates. Serve immediately with yogurt dressing. Yield: 4 servings.

PER SERVING: 252 CALORIES (29% FROM FAT)
FAT 8.2G (SATURATED FAT 2.5G)
PROTEIN 30.6G   CARBOHYDRATE 14.3G
CHOLESTEROL 83MG   SODIUM 228MG

HONEY-GLAZED HAM SLICES

¼ cup firmly packed brown sugar
¼ cup honey
¼ teaspoon dry mustard
3 whole cloves
4 (3-ounce) slices lean, lower-salt cooked ham
    (about ¼ inch thick)
Vegetable cooking spray
4 slices canned pineapple in juice, drained

Combine first 4 ingredients in a small saucepan; stir well. Bring to a boil over medium heat; boil 2 minutes, stirring occasionally. Remove and discard cloves, using a slotted spoon.

Arrange ham slices in an 11- x 7- x 1½-inch baking dish coated with cooking spray. Place 1 pineapple slice on each ham slice; spoon brown sugar mixture evenly over pineapple slices. Bake at 325° for 15 minutes or until thoroughly heated. Yield: 4 servings.

PER SERVING: 242 CALORIES (16% FROM FAT)
FAT 4.4G (SATURATED FAT 1.4G)
PROTEIN 15.4G CARBOHYDRATE 37.4G
CHOLESTEROL 42MG SODIUM 667MG

After the leg of pork is cured or smoked, it becomes ham. The package label identifies the type of processing and whether the ham has been cooked.

Ham labeled "fully cooked" does not require further heating and may be eaten cold. However, it will be more flavorful if heated to an internal temperature of 140°.

Ham marked "cook before eating" must be cooked to an internal temperature of 160°. If the package label does not specify whether it has been cooked, cook the ham to 160° to play it safe.

HAWAIIAN HAM KABOBS

1 (15¼-ounce) can pineapple chunks in juice, undrained
¼ cup low-sodium soy sauce
1 tablespoon brown sugar
1 tablespoon balsamic vinegar
2 teaspoons ground ginger
1 teaspoon garlic powder
1 teaspoon Dijon mustard
¼ teaspoon pepper
1 pound reduced-fat, lower-salt cooked ham, cut into 1-inch cubes
1 medium-size green pepper, cut into 1-inch pieces
1 medium-size sweet red pepper, cut into 1-inch pieces
Vegetable cooking spray
3 cups cooked long-grain rice (cooked without salt or fat)

Drain pineapple chunks, reserving juice. Set pineapple aside.

Combine juice, soy sauce, and next 6 ingredients in a shallow dish; stir well. Add ham and pineapple; stir gently to coat. Cover and marinate in refrigerator at least 15 minutes, stirring occasionally.

Remove ham and pineapple from marinade, reserving marinade. Place marinade in a small saucepan. Bring to a boil; reduce heat, and simmer 5 minutes.

Thread ham, pineapple, and peppers alternately onto 12 (10-inch) skewers. Coat grill rack with cooking spray; place on grill over medium-hot coals. Place kabobs on rack, and grill 8 to 10 minutes, turning and basting frequently with marinade. To serve, place ½ cup rice on each plate, and top with 2 kabobs. Yield: 6 servings.

PER SERVING: 272 CALORIES (14% FROM FAT)
FAT 4.3G (SATURATED FAT 1.3G)
PROTEIN 16.5G CARBOHYDRATE 41.9G
CHOLESTEROL 37MG SODIUM 873MG

Baking Directions: Prepare recipe as directed. Place ham kabobs in a 13- x 9- x 2-inch baking dish. Pour boiled marinade over kabobs. Bake, uncovered, at 350° for 15 minutes or until thoroughly heated.

Hawaiian Ham Kabobs

Lamb Steaks with Apricot Sauce (recipe on page 79)

LAMB & GAME

*W*hen you're looking for an entrée to break meal-time monotony, look to lamb. It is as versatile as beef and pork for both everyday and company meals.

If you're expecting a crowd, try Rosemary Roasted Lamb with Potatoes (page 76). For a smaller gathering, we recommend Lamb Steaks with Apricot Sauce (page 79). You can even cook lamb on the grill or in the wok—see Grilled Lamb Chops on page 82 and the two stir-fry recipes on page 85.

Another way to vary your menus is to include buffalo and venison (recipes begin on page 88). If you're not a hunter, you may be able to buy domesticated venison at large supermarkets or meat markets. Domesticated venison lacks much of the gamey taste of wild venison and is usually more tender.

Leg of Lamb à la Bonne Femme

1 (7½-pound) lean leg of lamb
3 cloves garlic, sliced
Vegetable cooking spray
8 black peppercorns
2 bay leaves
2 sprigs fresh parsley
1 teaspoon dried thyme
½ teaspoon dried marjoram
½ teaspoon dried sage
1½ pounds small round red potatoes
1¼ pounds small white boiling onions, peeled
1 (12-ounce) package baby carrots
5 stalks celery, cut into 1-inch pieces
1 teaspoon beef-flavored bouillon granules
1 cup boiling water
Fresh sage leaves (optional)

Trim fat from leg of lamb. Make several small slits on outside of lamb and insert garlic slices. Place lamb in a deep roasting pan coated with cooking spray. Insert meat thermometer into thickest part of lamb, being careful not to touch bone.

Combine peppercorns and next 5 ingredients on a small square of cheesecloth; bring ends together, and tie with string. Set herb bag aside.

Add potatoes, onions, carrots, and celery to pan. Combine bouillon granules and water; pour over lamb. Bake lamb, uncovered, at 325° for 2 hours. Add herb bag to pan, and bake an additional 30 minutes or until meat thermometer registers 150° (medium-rare) to 160° (medium), basting frequently with pan drippings.

Remove lamb from oven; discard herb bag. Let stand 10 minutes before carving. Garnish with fresh sage leaves, if desired. Yield: 15 servings.

PER SERVING: 236 CALORIES (27% FROM FAT)
FAT 7.2G (SATURATED FAT 2.6G)
PROTEIN 27.3G   CARBOHYDRATE 14.5G
CHOLESTEROL 81MG   SODIUM 150MG

Rosemary Roasted Lamb with Potatoes

Rosemary is a favorite seasoning for lamb. If the fresh herb is not available, use 2 teaspoons dried rosemary instead.

1 (3½-pound) lean boneless leg of lamb
6 cloves garlic, minced
2 tablespoons chopped fresh rosemary
½ teaspoon salt
Vegetable cooking spray
2¾ pounds small round red potatoes
1 teaspoon freshly ground pepper
1 cup water
Fresh rosemary sprigs (optional)

Trim fat from leg of lamb. Starting from center, slice horizontally through thickest part of lamb almost to, but not through, outer edge. Flip cut piece over to enlarge leg of lamb. Combine garlic, chopped rosemary, and salt; stir well. Rub half of garlic mixture over cut surface. Roll leg of lamb, and tie securely with string. Rub remaining garlic mixture over entire surface of lamb.

Place lamb on a rack in a roasting pan coated with cooking spray. Insert meat thermometer into thickest part of roast. Arrange potatoes around roast; sprinkle potatoes with pepper. Pour water into roasting pan. Bake lamb, uncovered, at 350° for 2 hours or until meat thermometer registers 150° (medium-rare) to 160° (medium).

To serve, transfer lamb to a serving platter, and remove string; arrange potatoes around lamb. Garnish with fresh rosemary sprigs, if desired. Yield: 14 servings.

PER SERVING: 236 CALORIES (26% FROM FAT)
FAT 6.8G (SATURATED FAT 2.4G)
PROTEIN 26.0G   CARBOHYDRATE 16.6G
CHOLESTEROL 76MG   SODIUM 147MG

LAMB WITH FRUIT AND NUT SAUCE

8 dried apricots, cut into strips
½ cup canned no-salt-added beef broth,
    undiluted
¼ cup currants
¼ cup brandy
4 (4-ounce) slices boneless leg of lamb
2 tablespoons all-purpose flour
Vegetable cooking spray
2 teaspoons vegetable oil
1 tablespoon chopped pecans, toasted
Flowering kale (optional)

Combine first 4 ingredients in a small bowl; stir well. Cover and chill at least 8 hours.

Trim fat from lamb. Place lamb between 2 sheets of heavy-duty plastic wrap, and flatten to ½-inch thickness, using a meat mallet or rolling pin; dredge in flour.

Coat a nonstick skillet with cooking spray; add oil. Place over medium-high heat until hot. Add lamb; cook 5 minutes on each side or until lightly browned. Add apricot mixture and pecans; cover, reduce heat, and simmer 15 minutes or until lamb is tender. Transfer lamb to a platter lined with kale, if desired; spoon apricot mixture over lamb. Yield: 4 servings.

PER SERVING: 271 CALORIES (28% FROM FAT)
FAT 8.5G (SATURATED FAT 2.1G)
PROTEIN 21.8G   CARBOHYDRATE 18.3G
CHOLESTEROL 64MG   SODIUM 68MG

Lamb with Fruit and Nut Sauce

Minted Lamb Steaks with Onion

MINTED LAMB STEAKS WITH ONION

6 (4-ounce) lean lamb sirloin steaks
2 medium-size purple onions, thinly sliced
1 cup red wine vinegar
3 tablespoons minced fresh mint
½ teaspoon pepper
2 tablespoons sugar
¾ cup canned no-salt-added chicken broth,
     undiluted
Vegetable cooking spray
Fresh mint sprigs (optional)

Trim fat from steaks; place steaks and onion in a shallow dish. Combine vinegar, minced mint, and pepper; pour over steaks and onion. Cover and marinate in refrigerator 1 hour.

Remove steaks and onion from marinade; reserve

marinade. Combine marinade and sugar in a small saucepan; bring to a boil. Reduce heat, and simmer until mixture is reduced by half. Add broth, and cook until mixture is reduced to about ½ cup. Set aside, and keep warm.

Place onion on rack of a broiler pan coated with cooking spray; place steaks on top of onion. Broil 5½ inches from heat (with electric oven door partially opened) 6 minutes on each side or to desired degree of doneness. To serve, drizzle broth mixture evenly over steaks and onion. Garnish with mint sprigs, if desired. Yield: 6 servings.

PER SERVING: 226 CALORIES (33% FROM FAT)
FAT 8.3G (SATURATED FAT 2.8G)
PROTEIN 25.2G   CARBOHYDRATE 10.1G
CHOLESTEROL 78MG   SODIUM 82MG

LAMB STEAKS WITH APRICOT SAUCE

(pictured on page 74)

8 (5-ounce) lean lamb sirloin steaks (¾ inch thick)
½ cup no-sugar-added apricot spread
2 tablespoons unsweetened orange juice
Vegetable cooking spray
Apricot Sauce
Fresh hot peppers (optional)

Trim fat from steaks; set aside.

Combine apricot spread and orange juice in a small saucepan; cook over medium-low heat until spread melts, stirring occasionally.

Coat grill rack with cooking spray; place on grill over medium-hot coals (350° to 400°). Place steaks on rack, and grill, uncovered, 5 minutes on each side or to desired degree of doneness, basting occasionally with apricot spread mixture. Serve with Apricot Sauce. Garnish with fresh hot peppers, if desired. Yield: 8 servings.

APRICOT SAUCE
1 (16-ounce) can apricot halves in juice, undrained
1 tablespoon white wine vinegar
2 teaspoons cornstarch
2 tablespoons thinly sliced canned jalapeño peppers, seeded

Drain apricots, reserving juice; quarter apricot halves, and set aside.

Combine reserved apricot juice, vinegar, and cornstarch in a small saucepan. Bring to a boil; reduce heat, and simmer, stirring constantly, 1 minute or until thickened. Remove from heat. Stir in apricots and jalapeño pepper. Yield: 1¾ cups.

PER SERVING: 241 CALORIES (30% FROM FAT)
FAT 8.0G (SATURATED FAT 2.8G)
PROTEIN 24.5G   CARBOHYDRATE 16.6G
CHOLESTEROL 78MG   SODIUM 100MG

LAMB CHOPS WITH APPLES AND PRUNES

Nafplion olives are small green olives marinated in brine. Substitute any type of Greek olive if Nafplion are not available.

8 (5-ounce) lean lamb loin chops (1 inch thick)
Butter-flavored vegetable cooking spray
2 teaspoons reduced-calorie margarine
1 cup peeled, finely chopped Granny Smith apple
¾ cup chopped onion
1 cup water
1 (8-ounce) can no-salt-added tomato sauce
1 tablespoon all-purpose flour
1 tablespoon chopped fresh rosemary
1½ teaspoons chopped fresh oregano
1½ teaspoons chopped fresh marjoram
1 teaspoon coarsely ground pepper
16 Nafplion olives
16 pitted prunes
2 tablespoons dry sherry

Trim fat from chops. Coat a large nonstick skillet with cooking spray; place over medium-high heat until hot. Add chops; cook 2 to 3 minutes on each side or until browned. Remove chops from skillet. Drain and pat dry with paper towels. Place chops in an ovenproof Dutch oven; set aside. Wipe drippings from skillet with a paper towel.

Melt margarine in skillet over medium-high heat. Add apple and onion; sauté 3 minutes or until tender. Combine water and next 6 ingredients, stirring well; add to apple mixture in skillet. Bring to a boil, stirring constantly. Pour over lamb.

Cover and bake lamb at 350° for 30 minutes. Add olives, prunes, and sherry. Cover and bake an additional 25 minutes or to desired degree of doneness.

To serve, place a chop on each individual serving plate. Spoon sauce mixture evenly over chops. Yield: 8 servings.

PER SERVING: 259 CALORIES (30% FROM FAT)
FAT 8.5G (SATURATED FAT 2.6G)
PROTEIN 25.1G   CARBOHYDRATE 20.4G
CHOLESTEROL 76MG   SODIUM 191MG

LAMB CHOPS MARSALA

4 (4-ounce) lean lamb loin chops
Vegetable cooking spray
½ cup water
½ cup Marsala
2 tablespoons tomato paste
1 cup sliced fresh mushrooms
¼ cup chopped onion

Trim fat from chops. Coat a large skillet with cooking spray; place over medium-high heat until hot. Add chops, and cook 4 minutes on each side or to desired degree of doneness. Remove chops from skillet; drain on paper towels, and keep warm. Wipe drippings from skillet with a paper towel.

Combine water, wine, and tomato paste in a bowl; stir well with a wire whisk until mixture is smooth. Add wine mixture, mushrooms, and onion to skillet; cook over high heat, stirring constantly, 2 minutes or until thickened. Spoon sauce over chops. Yield: 2 servings.

PER SERVING: 199 CALORIES (33% FROM FAT)
FAT 7.4G (SATURATED FAT 2.5G)
PROTEIN 25.4G   CARBOHYDRATE 7.4G
CHOLESTEROL 75MG   SODIUM 95MG

TERIYAKI LAMB CHOPS

4 (5-ounce) lean lamb loin chops (1 inch thick)
½ cup dry sherry
¼ cup firmly packed brown sugar
¼ cup low-sodium soy sauce
2 tablespoons water
1 tablespoon peeled, minced gingerroot
Vegetable cooking spray

Trim fat from chops. Place chops in a large heavy-duty, zip-top plastic bag. Combine sherry and next 4 ingredients; stir well. Pour over chops. Seal bag; shake until chops are well coated. Marinate in refrigerator 8 hours, turning bag occasionally.

Remove chops from marinade. Place marinade in a small saucepan. Bring to a boil; reduce heat, and simmer 2 minutes.

Coat grill rack with cooking spray; place on grill over medium-hot coals. Place chops on rack, and grill 7 to 9 minutes on each side or to desired degree of doneness, basting occasionally with marinade. Yield: 4 servings.

PER SERVING: 257 CALORIES (31% FROM FAT)
FAT 8.8G (SATURATED FAT 3.1G)
PROTEIN 26.6G   CARBOHYDRATE 14.6G
CHOLESTEROL 84MG   SODIUM 471MG

RASPBERRY-MINT CHOPS

Ask your butcher for French-cut rib chops, which are cut from a trimmed rack of lamb.

3 tablespoons seedless red raspberry jam
2 tablespoons lemon juice
2 teaspoons minced fresh mint
4 (4-ounce) French-cut lamb rib chops
Vegetable cooking spray
Kiwifruit slices (optional)
Fresh mint sprigs (optional)
Fresh raspberries (optional)

Combine first 3 ingredients in a small saucepan; stir well. Bring to a boil over medium heat; reduce heat, and simmer 2½ minutes or until mixture is reduced to ¼ cup. Set aside, and keep warm.

Trim fat from chops. Coat a skillet with cooking spray, and place over medium heat until hot. Add chops; cook 4 minutes on each side or to desired degree of doneness. Place on serving plates; spoon 2 tablespoons sauce over each chop. If desired, garnish with kiwifruit slices, mint sprigs, and raspberries. Yield: 2 servings.

PER SERVING: 241 CALORIES (27% FROM FAT)
FAT 7.2G (SATURATED FAT 3.2G)
PROTEIN 26.0G   CARBOHYDRATE 16.1G
CHOLESTEROL 62MG   SODIUM 58MG

Raspberry-Mint Chops

GRILLED LAMB CHOPS

4 (5-ounce) lean lamb loin chops (1 inch thick)
½ cup frozen apple juice concentrate, thawed
   and undiluted
½ teaspoon curry powder
½ teaspoon ground cumin
¼ teaspoon garlic powder
Vegetable cooking spray
Edible flowers (optional)

Trim fat from chops. Place chops in a heavy-duty, zip-top plastic bag. Combine apple juice concentrate and next 3 ingredients; stir well. Pour marinade over chops; seal bag, and shake until chops are well coated. Marinate meat in refrigerator 6 to 8 hours, turning bag occasionally to coat meat.

Remove lamb from marinade. Place marinade in a small saucepan. Bring to a boil; reduce heat, and simmer 5 minutes. Set aside.

Coat grill rack with cooking spray; place on grill over medium-hot coals. Place chops on rack, and grill 7 to 9 minutes on each side or to desired degree of doneness, basting chops frequently with marinade. Garnish with edible flowers, if desired. Yield: 4 servings.

PER SERVING: 253 CALORIES (32% FROM FAT)
FAT 9.0G (SATURATED FAT 3.1G)
PROTEIN 26.8G   CARBOHYDRATE 14.8G
CHOLESTEROL 84MG   SODIUM 84MG

Grilled Lamb Chops

LAMB STROGANOFF

For this variation of the traditional beef stroganoff, we used a mere teaspoon of oil for sautéing and used low-fat sour cream.

Olive oil-flavored vegetable cooking spray
1½ pounds lean boneless lamb, cut into
   1½-inch cubes
4½ cups sliced fresh mushrooms
1 teaspoon olive oil
1 cup sliced green onions
1 clove garlic, minced
1½ tablespoons all-purpose flour
1 tablespoon no-salt-added tomato paste
1 (13¾-ounce) can no-salt-added beef broth,
   divided
4 thin lemon slices
½ cup low-fat sour cream
2 teaspoons all-purpose flour
¼ teaspoon salt
¾ cup chopped fresh parsley
3 cups cooked wide egg noodles (cooked
   without salt or fat)

Coat a large nonstick skillet with cooking spray; place over medium-high heat until hot. Add lamb; cook 5 minutes or until browned on all sides, stirring often. Drain and pat dry with paper towels. Wipe drippings from skillet with a paper towel.

Coat skillet with cooking spray, and place over medium-high heat until hot. Add mushrooms; sauté 5 minutes. Remove from skillet, and set aside.

Add oil to skillet; place over medium-high heat until hot. Add green onions; sauté 2 minutes. Add garlic; sauté 30 seconds.

Combine 1½ tablespoons flour, tomato paste, and 2 tablespoons beef broth in a medium bowl, stirring well with a wire whisk. Add remaining broth, stirring until smooth.

Add broth mixture to onion mixture. Cook over medium heat, stirring constantly, until slightly thickened. Return lamb to skillet; cover, reduce heat, and simmer 45 minutes, stirring occasionally. Add lemon slices; cook, uncovered, 15 minutes. Add sautéed mushrooms; cook 10 minutes. Remove from heat; remove and discard lemon slices.

Combine sour cream, 2 teaspoons flour, and salt, stirring well. Stir sour cream mixture and parsley into lamb mixture; serve immediately over hot cooked noodles. Yield: 6 servings.

PER SERVING: 324 CALORIES (28% FROM FAT)
FAT 9.9G (SATURATED FAT 3.7G)
PROTEIN 29.7G   CARBOHYDRATE 27.6G
CHOLESTEROL 107MG   SODIUM 190MG

LAMB DIANE

1 pound lean boneless lamb
½ teaspoon cracked pepper
¼ cup plus 2 tablespoons dry red wine
2 tablespoons lemon juice
1½ tablespoons low-sodium Worcestershire
   sauce
1½ teaspoons cornstarch
Vegetable cooking spray
1 teaspoon vegetable oil
¼ cup finely chopped shallots
2 cloves garlic, minced
2 tablespoons minced fresh parsley
2 tablespoons minced fresh chives
2 cups cooked long-grain rice (cooked without
   salt or fat)

Trim fat from lamb; cut lamb into thin strips, and sprinkle with pepper. Set aside. Combine wine and next 3 ingredients in a bowl; stir well. Set aside.

Coat a wok or large nonstick skillet with cooking spray; add oil. Heat at medium-high (375°) until hot. Add lamb, and stir-fry 5 minutes. Remove lamb from wok. Drain and pat dry with paper towels. Wipe drippings from wok with a paper towel.

Coat wok with cooking spray; place over medium-high heat until hot. Add shallots and garlic; stir-fry 1 minute. Return lamb to wok. Add reserved wine mixture. Cook, stirring constantly, until mixture is thickened and thoroughly heated. Stir in parsley and chives. Spoon lamb mixture over cooked rice. Yield: 4 servings.

PER SERVING: 332 CALORIES (25% FROM FAT)
FAT 9.4G (SATURATED FAT 3.0G)
PROTEIN 26.6G   CARBOHYDRATE 33.3G
CHOLESTEROL 74MG   SODIUM 93MG

Spicy Orange Lamb Stir-Fry

SPICY ORANGE LAMB STIR-FRY

1 pound lamb cutlets
¼ cup water
3 tablespoons dry sherry
2 tablespoons reduced-sodium soy sauce
1 teaspoon sugar
½ teaspoon dried crushed red pepper
2 teaspoons cornstarch
Vegetable cooking spray
1 teaspoon vegetable oil
1 (8-ounce) can water chestnuts, drained
1 medium-size sweet red pepper, seeded and cut into cubes
4 green onions, cut into 1-inch pieces
1 tablespoon grated orange rind
1 tablespoon peeled, minced gingerroot
2 cups cooked long-grain rice (cooked without salt or fat)

Trim fat from cutlets; cut cutlets into thin strips, and set aside. Combine water, sherry, soy sauce, sugar, and crushed red pepper in a large bowl. Stir well. Add lamb strips. Cover and let stand 20 minutes.

Drain lamb, reserving marinade. Combine marinade and cornstarch, stirring until smooth. Set mixture aside.

Coat a wok or skillet with cooking spray; add oil. Heat at medium-high (375°) for 2 minutes. Add lamb; stir-fry 5 minutes. Remove lamb from wok, and set aside. Add water chestnuts and next 4 ingredients to wok; stir-fry 1 minute. Return lamb to wok. Add reserved marinade. Cook, stirring constantly, until mixture is thickened; spoon over cooked rice. Yield: 4 servings.

PER SERVING: 317 CALORIES (21% FROM FAT)
FAT 7.5G (SATURATED FAT 2.4G)
PROTEIN 26.2G CARBOHYDRATE 34.7G
CHOLESTEROL 74MG SODIUM 324MG

MANDARIN LAMB STIR-FRY

4 (4-ounce) lamb cutlets (½ inch thick)
¼ cup water
3 tablespoons vinegar
2 tablespoons reduced-sodium soy sauce
2 teaspoons brown sugar
1 teaspoon cornstarch
¼ teaspoon ground coriander
¼ teaspoon ground red pepper
Vegetable cooking spray
1 teaspoon vegetable oil
1 medium-size sweet red pepper, seeded and cut into strips
1 cup sliced celery
1 cup cubed fresh pineapple
1 cup cauliflower flowerets
3 cups cooked long-grain rice (cooked without salt or fat)

Trim fat from cutlets; cut into thin strips, and set aside. Combine water and next 6 ingredients; stir until smooth. Set aside.

Coat a wok or large nonstick skillet with cooking spray; add oil. Heat at medium-high (375°) for 2 minutes. Add lamb; stir-fry 5 minutes. Remove lamb from wok, and set aside. Add sweet red pepper, celery, pineapple, and cauliflower to wok; stir-fry 1 minute. Add lamb and reserved vinegar mixture. Cook, stirring constantly, until thickened. Serve over cooked rice. Yield: 6 servings.

PER SERVING: 253 CALORIES (18% FROM FAT)
FAT 5.2G (SATURATED FAT 1.6G)
PROTEIN 18.1G CARBOHYDRATE 32.1G
CHOLESTEROL 49MG SODIUM 203MG

Did You Know?

Although only a small amount of oil is needed for these stir-fries, choose one that doesn't smoke at high temperatures, such as peanut, safflower, or corn oil.

MOROCCAN LAMB WITH COUSCOUS

1 pound lean ground lamb
½ cup soft breadcrumbs
½ cup finely chopped onion
½ cup chopped fresh parsley
½ teaspoon ground coriander
⅛ teaspoon salt
⅛ teaspoon black pepper
Dash of ground cinnamon
Dash of ground nutmeg
Vegetable cooking spray
½ teaspoon garlic powder
¼ teaspoon salt
¼ teaspoon ground cumin
¼ teaspoon chili powder
¼ teaspoon ground red pepper
2 (14½-ounce) cans no-salt-added whole
    tomatoes, undrained and chopped
3½ cups water
2⅔ cups couscous, uncooked
¾ cup chopped dried apricot halves
½ cup dried currants

Combine first 9 ingredients in a bowl, and stir well. Divide mixture evenly into 32 meatballs. Coat a large nonstick skillet with cooking spray; place over medium-high heat until hot. Add meatballs, and cook 8 minutes or until browned on all sides. Drain and pat dry with paper towels. Set aside, and keep warm. Wipe drippings from skillet with paper towels.

Combine garlic powder and next 5 ingredients in skillet, and bring to a boil. Reduce heat, and simmer, uncovered, 5 minutes. Remove from heat, and set aside.

Bring water to a boil in a large saucepan, and stir in couscous. Remove from heat, and let stand, covered, 5 minutes; fluff with a fork. Stir in apricots and currants.

To serve, arrange couscous and meatballs on a platter; top with tomato mixture. Yield: 8 servings.

PER SERVING: 250 CALORIES (17% FROM FAT)
FAT 4.8G (SATURATED FAT 1.6G)
PROTEIN 17.3G   CARBOHYDRATE 35.7G
CHOLESTEROL 40MG   SODIUM 190MG

LAMB AND SPINACH PILAF

2 cups canned no-salt-added beef broth,
    undiluted
1 cup bulgur (cracked wheat), uncooked
¼ teaspoon salt
1 pound lean ground lamb
1 cup chopped onion
½ cup raisins
½ cup water
2 tablespoons lemon juice
½ teaspoon ground cinnamon
¼ teaspoon salt
¼ teaspoon pepper
¼ teaspoon ground nutmeg
1 (10-ounce) package washed and trimmed
    fresh spinach, chopped

Bring broth to a boil in a medium saucepan; add bulgur and ¼ teaspoon salt. Cover, reduce heat, and simmer 15 minutes or until bulgur is tender and liquid is absorbed. Set aside, and keep warm.

Cook lamb in a large Dutch oven over medium heat until browned, stirring until it crumbles. Drain and pat dry with paper towels. Wipe drippings from pan with a paper towel.

Return lamb to pan; add onion and next 7 ingredients. Bring to a boil; cover, reduce heat, and simmer 7 minutes. Add spinach; cover and simmer an additional 3 minutes or until spinach wilts.

Divide bulgur mixture evenly among 6 individual serving plates. Top each serving with ⅔ cup lamb mixture. Yield: 6 servings.

PER SERVING: 269 CALORIES (20% FROM FAT)
FAT 6.1G (SATURATED FAT 2.1G)
PROTEIN 22.1G   CARBOHYDRATE 32.7G
CHOLESTEROL 54MG   SODIUM 289MG

Lamb and Spinach Pilaf

Pot Roast of Venison with Prune Sauce

POT ROAST OF VENISON WITH PRUNE SAUCE

Vegetable cooking spray
2 teaspoons olive oil
1 medium onion, thinly sliced
¾ cup chopped celery (about 1 large stalk)
½ cup thinly sliced carrot (about 1 medium)
3 cloves garlic, minced
1½ cups water
1½ cups dry red wine
1 tablespoon Worcestershire sauce
2 teaspoons dried thyme
1 teaspoon dried savory
15 juniper berries, crushed
3 bay leaves
1 (1½-pound) boneless leg of venison
12 small red potatoes
12 fresh pearl onions, peeled (about ½ pound)
Prune Sauce

Coat a large nonstick skillet with cooking spray; add olive oil, and place over medium-high heat until hot. Add sliced onion and next 3 ingredients; sauté until tender. Combine onion mixture, water, and next 6 ingredients in a large, shallow dish; set aside.

Trim fat from roast; add roast to onion mixture, turning to coat. Cover and marinate in refrigerator 8 hours, turning frequently.

Place roast in a large Dutch oven, reserving marinade. Insert meat thermometer into center of roast. Pour marinade over roast; place onion mixture, potatoes, and pearl onions around roast.

Bake at 325° for 1 hour or until meat thermometer registers 140° (medium-rare), basting frequently with marinade. Place roast on a serving platter. Remove vegetables from Dutch oven with a slotted spoon, and place around roast. Discard bay leaves and remaining cooking liquid. Cut roast into slices; serve with Prune Sauce. Yield: 6 servings.

PRUNE SAUCE

¼ cup dry white wine
1 tablespoon all-purpose flour
½ cup water
¼ cup plus 2 tablespoons prune juice
¼ teaspoon beef-flavored bouillon granules

Combine wine and flour in a small saucepan; stir well. Add remaining ingredients; bring to a boil, and cook 1 minute or until thickened, stirring occasionally. Serve warm. Yield: 1 cup.

PER SERVING: 323 CALORIES (15% FROM FAT)
FAT 5.5G (SATURATED FAT 1.7G)
PROTEIN 37.6G   CARBOHYDRATE 30.0G
CHOLESTEROL 127MG   SODIUM 143MG

VENISON POT ROAST WITH VEGETABLES

3 pounds venison roast
3 tablespoons all-purpose flour
½ teaspoon salt
½ teaspoon pepper
Vegetable cooking spray
1 tablespoon vegetable oil
1 medium onion, sliced
1 cup apple cider
1 cup canned no-salt-added beef broth, undiluted
1 teaspoon dried thyme
1 bay leaf
8 small round red potatoes, peeled
6 carrots, scraped and quartered
4 stalks celery, cut into 2-inch pieces

Trim fat from roast. Combine flour, salt, and pepper in a dish; stir well. Dredge roast in flour mixture.
Coat a large Dutch oven with cooking spray; add oil. Place over medium-high heat until hot. Add roast; cook 5 minutes or until browned on all sides. Add onion, cider, broth, thyme, and bay leaf to Dutch oven. Bring mixture to a boil; cover, reduce heat, and simmer 1 hour and 45 minutes.

Add potatoes, carrot, and celery to Dutch oven; cover and simmer 45 minutes or until roast and vegetables are tender. Transfer roast to a serving platter; spoon vegetables around roast, using a slotted spoon. Remove and discard bay leaf. Spoon remaining mixture in pan over roast and vegetables. Yield: 8 servings.

PER SERVING: 269 CALORIES (18% FROM FAT)
FAT 5.3G (SATURATED FAT 1.6G)
PROTEIN 32.7G   CARBOHYDRATE 21.5G
CHOLESTEROL 113MG   SODIUM 247MG

MARINATED VENISON STEAKS

6 (4-ounce) lean boneless venison loin steaks (½ inch thick)
¼ cup dry red wine
1½ tablespoons low-sodium soy sauce
¾ teaspoon dried thyme
¼ teaspoon salt
¼ teaspoon pepper
¼ teaspoon hot sauce
1 clove garlic, minced
1 bay leaf
Vegetable cooking spray

Trim fat from steaks; place steaks in a heavy-duty, zip-top plastic bag. Combine wine and next 7 ingredients; stir well. Pour over steaks; seal bag, and shake until steaks are well coated. Marinate in refrigerator 8 hours, turning bag occasionally.
Remove steaks from marinade. Place marinade in a saucepan, and bring to a boil; set aside. Remove and discard bay leaf. Coat grill rack with cooking spray; place on grill over medium-hot coals. Place steaks on rack, and grill 3 minutes on each side or to desired degree of doneness, basting occasionally with marinade. Yield: 6 servings.

PER SERVING: 133 CALORIES (19% FROM FAT)
FAT 2.8G (SATURATED FAT 1.0G)
PROTEIN 24.8G   CARBOHYDRATE 0.4G
CHOLESTEROL 92MG   SODIUM 209MG

Venison Meat Loaf

VENISON MEAT LOAF

1 pound lean ground venison
¾ cup wheat bran flakes cereal, lightly
    crushed
1 cup finely shredded carrot (about 1 medium)
½ cup chopped onion
3 tablespoons no-salt-added vegetable juice
2 egg whites
2 tablespoons all-purpose flour
2 tablespoons chopped fresh parsley
½ teaspoon pepper
¼ teaspoon salt
¼ teaspoon beef-flavored bouillon granules
⅛ teaspoon dry mustard
½ teaspoon dried marjoram, divided
½ teaspoon dried rosemary, divided
Vegetable cooking spray
3 tablespoons no-salt-added reduced-calorie
    ketchup

Combine first 12 ingredients, ¼ teaspoon marjoram, and ¼ teaspoon rosemary in a medium bowl; stir well. Shape into a loaf, and place in an 8½- x 4½- x 2½-inch loafdish coated with cooking spray.

Combine ketchup, remaining ¼ teaspoon marjoram, and remaining ¼ teaspoon rosemary. Spread 1 tablespoon of ketchup mixture over meat loaf.

Bake meat loaf at 350° for 1 hour and 15 minutes. Let stand in pan 10 minutes. Place meat loaf on a serving platter, ketchup side up, and spread with remaining ketchup mixture. Cut meat loaf into 12 slices. Yield: 6 servings.

PER SERVING: 143 CALORIES (14% FROM FAT)
FAT 2.2G (SATURATED FAT 0.8G)
PROTEIN 19.5G   CARBOHYDRATE 10.6G
CHOLESTEROL 64MG   SODIUM 276MG

BUFFALO STEAKS

1 (1-pound) top sirloin buffalo steak (½ inch
    thick)
1¼ teaspoons ground cumin
¼ teaspoon salt
¼ teaspoon pepper
Vegetable cooking spray
1 cup Jalapeño-Fruit Sauce (page 134)

Trim fat from steak; cut steak into 4 equal pieces. Place steak between 2 sheets of heavy-duty plastic wrap, and flatten to ⅜-inch thickness, using a meat mallet or rolling pin. Combine cumin, salt, and pepper; rub mixture onto both sides of steaks.

Coat a medium nonstick skillet with cooking spray; place over medium heat until hot. Add steaks; cook 4 minutes on each side or to desired degree of doneness. Serve each steak with ¼ cup Jalapeño-Fruit Sauce. Yield: 4 servings.

PER SERVING: 170 CALORIES (12% FROM FAT)
FAT 2.2G (SATURATED FAT 0.6G)
PROTEIN 24.2G   CARBOHYDRATE 14.3G
CHOLESTEROL 50MG   SODIUM 417MG

BUFFALO BURGERS

2 teaspoons vegetable oil
1 cup finely chopped onion
1 pound lean ground buffalo or ground round
1 teaspoon minced fresh thyme
½ teaspoon salt
½ teaspoon pepper
1 egg, lightly beaten
Vegetable cooking spray
½ cup dry vermouth
4 (1½-ounce) hamburger buns, split
4 lettuce leaves
4 tomato slices
4 onion slices

Heat oil in a large nonstick skillet over medium-high heat. Add 1 cup onion; sauté until tender.

Combine sautéed onion, meat, thyme, salt, pepper, and egg in a bowl, and stir well. Divide the meat mixture into 4 equal portions, shaping each into a 3½-inch patty.

Coat skillet with cooking spray, and place over medium-high heat until hot. Add patties; cook 3 minutes. Turn; reduce heat to medium-low, and cook 1 minute. Add vermouth; cover and cook an additional 2 minutes. Serve patties on buns with lettuce, tomato, and onion. Yield: 4 servings.

PER SERVING: 331 CALORIES (25% FROM FAT)
FAT 9.1G (SATURATED FAT 1.9G)
PROTEIN 29.3G   CARBOHYDRATE 31.3G
CHOLESTEROL 122MG   SODIUM 496MG

Appetizer Meatballs (recipe on page 95)

SNACKS & SANDWICHES

*A*lthough preparing and serving sandwiches is easy, making them healthy is not. You have to be careful in your selection of sandwich ingredients because so many of them are high in fat.

Snacks and appetizers pose a similar problem. Chips, dips, crackers, and cheese often push the fat above recommended amounts.

Don't despair! By using nonfat mayonnaise, mustard, chutney, and other low-fat ingredients, you can create any number of appetizers, snacks, and sandwiches to fit your low-fat menu plans. Even a Triple Treat Burger (page 103) gets only 25 percent of its calories from fat. And Layered Diablo Dip (page 94) scales in at under 30 percent fat. It also includes a bonus recipe for low-fat tortilla chips.

Layered Diablo Dip

LAYERED DIABLO DIP

Vegetable cooking spray
6 ounces ground round
6 ounces freshly ground raw turkey
½ cup chopped onion
1 (16-ounce) can pinto beans, drained and
    mashed
1 teaspoon chili powder
½ teaspoon ground cumin
1 (4-ounce) can chopped green chiles,
    undrained
½ cup (2 ounces) shredded reduced-fat
    Monterey Jack cheese
½ cup (2 ounces) shredded reduced-fat
    Cheddar cheese
¾ cup no-salt-added picante sauce
½ cup nonfat sour cream
¼ cup sliced green onions
Corn Tortilla Chips

Coat a nonstick skillet with cooking spray; place over medium-high heat until hot. Add ground round, turkey, and chopped onion; cook until meat is browned, stirring until it crumbles. Drain meat mixture, and pat dry with paper towels; set aside.

Combine beans, chili powder, and cumin; stir well. Spread bean mixture in a shallow 1½-quart baking dish coated with cooking spray; layer meat mixture, green chiles, cheeses, and picante sauce over bean mixture. Bake, uncovered, at 350° for 20 minutes or until cheese melts and mixture is thoroughly heated.

Top dip evenly with sour cream and green onions. Serve with Corn Tortilla Chips. Yield: 24 appetizer servings.

CORN TORTILLA CHIPS
2 cups water
9 (6-inch) corn tortillas

Pour water into a shallow baking dish. Working with 1 tortilla at a time, dip tortilla into water for 2 seconds. Drain and cut tortilla into 8 wedges. Repeat procedure with remaining tortillas.

Place one-third of tortilla wedges in a single layer on an ungreased baking sheet. Bake at 350° for 15 minutes or until crisp and lightly browned. Remove chips from baking sheet; let cool on wire racks. Repeat procedure with remaining tortillas. Yield: 6 dozen chips.

PER SERVING: 90 CALORIES (29% FROM FAT)
FAT 2.9G (SATURATED FAT 1.1G)
PROTEIN 6.2G   CARBOHYDRATE 10.2G
CHOLESTEROL 11MG   SODIUM 182MG

APPETIZER MEATBALLS
(pictured on page 92)

1 pound ground round
½ cup soft breadcrumbs
2 tablespoons chopped green pepper
2 tablespoons skim milk
1 teaspoon low-sodium Worcestershire sauce
2 egg whites, lightly beaten
Vegetable cooking spray
1 tablespoon plus 1 teaspoon cornstarch
¼ cup water
¼ cup firmly packed brown sugar
¼ cup red wine vinegar
¼ cup low-sodium soy sauce
1 teaspoon peeled, minced gingerroot
⅛ teaspoon garlic powder

Combine first 6 ingredients in a large bowl; stir well. Shape mixture into 42 (1-inch) meatballs. Arrange meatballs on rack of a broiler pan coated with cooking spray. Broil 5½ inches from heat (with electric oven door partially opened) 10 minutes or until browned, turning frequently.

Combine cornstarch and water in a large saucepan; stir well. Add brown sugar and remaining ingredients; stir well. Place over medium heat; bring to a boil, stirring constantly. Reduce heat, and simmer, stirring constantly, 3 to 5 minutes or until thickened. Add meatballs, stirring gently to

coat. Transfer to a chafing dish, and serve warm. Yield: 3½ dozen appetizers.

PER APPETIZER: 23 CALORIES (23% FROM FAT)
FAT 0.6G (SATURATED FAT 0.2G)
PROTEIN 2.6G   CARBOHYDRATE 1.5G
CHOLESTEROL 6MG   SODIUM 50MG

PASTRY BEEF ROLLS

¼ cup nonfat mayonnaise
1½ teaspoons prepared horseradish
1 teaspoon balsamic vinegar
6 green onions
6 sheets frozen phyllo pastry, thawed
Vegetable cooking spray
1 tablespoon sesame seeds, toasted
6 very thin slices lean roast beef

Combine first 3 ingredients in a small bowl, stirring well. Set aside. Cut each green onion to measure 7 inches; reserve remaining ends of green onions for other uses. Set green onions aside.

Place 1 sheet of phyllo on a damp towel (keep remaining phyllo covered). Lightly coat phyllo with cooking spray. Fold phyllo in half crosswise, bringing short ends together. Lightly coat with cooking spray. Fold in half again crosswise, bringing short ends together. Lightly coat with cooking spray.

Spread 2 teaspoons mayonnaise mixture over phyllo to within ½ inch of edges. Sprinkle ½ teaspoon sesame seeds over mayonnaise mixture. Top with 1 beef slice. Place 1 green onion in center, parallel with long edge. Roll up phyllo, jellyroll fashion, starting with long side; tuck ends under.

Place, seam side down, on a baking sheet coated with cooking spray. Lightly coat top of pastry with cooking spray. Repeat procedure with remaining phyllo, mayonnaise mixture, sesame seeds, beef slices, and onions. Bake at 400° for 15 minutes or until rolls are crisp. Cut each into thirds. Serve immediately. Yield: 1½ dozen appetizers.

PER APPETIZER: 41 CALORIES (26% FROM FAT)
FAT 1.2G (SATURATED FAT 0.3G)
PROTEIN 2.3G   CARBOHYDRATE 5.4G
CHOLESTEROL 6MG   SODIUM 89MG

PORK SATÉ

This favorite Indonesian dish may be enjoyed as a snack, appetizer, or entrée. If using wooden skewers, soak them in water 30 minutes before grilling.

2 (1-pound) pork tenderloins
½ cup low-sodium chicken broth, undiluted
¼ cup creamy peanut butter
¼ cup honey
¼ cup hoisin sauce
2 tablespoons minced fresh cilantro
2 tablespoons low-sodium soy sauce
1 teaspoon dark sesame oil
½ teaspoon dried crushed red pepper
1 clove garlic, minced
¼ cup water
Vegetable cooking spray

Trim fat from pork; cut each tenderloin lengthwise into 12 equal strips. Thread strips onto 24 (6-inch) skewers; place in a shallow nonmetal dish. Combine broth and next 8 ingredients; stir well with a wire whisk. Reserve ¾ cup peanut butter mixture; set aside. Add water to remaining peanut butter mixture; pour over kabobs, turning to coat. Cover and marinate in refrigerator 30 minutes, turning occasionally.

Remove kabobs from marinade, reserving marinade. Bring marinade to a boil; set aside.

Coat grill rack with cooking spray, and place on grill over medium-hot coals (350° to 400°). Place kabobs on rack; grill 6 minutes on each side or until done, basting occasionally with reserved marinade. Serve kabobs with reserved ¾ cup peanut butter sauce. Yield: 2 dozen appetizers.

PER APPETIZER: 82 CALORIES (33% FROM FAT)
FAT 3.0G (SATURATED FAT 0.7G)
PROTEIN 9.1G   CARBOHYDRATE 4.8G
CHOLESTEROL 26MG   SODIUM 144MG

INDIVIDUAL PESTO PIZZAS

¼ cup lightly packed fresh basil
1 clove garlic
2 cups torn fresh spinach
2 tablespoons grated Parmesan cheese
2 teaspoons lemon juice
2 whole wheat English muffins, split and toasted
2 (½-ounce) slices Canadian bacon, cut into very thin strips
3 tablespoons (¾ ounce) shredded nonfat mozzarella cheese
2 teaspoons sliced green onions

Position knife blade in food processor bowl; drop basil and garlic through food chute with processor running, and process 15 seconds or until minced. Add spinach, Parmesan cheese, and lemon juice; process 30 seconds or until smooth, scraping sides of processor bowl once.

Spread spinach mixture evenly over muffin halves. Divide Canadian bacon strips evenly among muffin halves. Broil 5½ inches from heat (with electric oven door partially opened) 1 minute. Sprinkle evenly with mozzarella cheese; broil an additional minute or until cheese melts. Sprinkle with green onions. Serve immediately. Yield: 4 servings.

PER SERVING: 123 CALORIES (15% FROM FAT)
FAT 2.0G (SATURATED FAT 1.0G)
PROTEIN 7.4G   CARBOHYDRATE 18.9G
CHOLESTEROL 7MG   SODIUM 362MG

Did You Know?

Pesto is an uncooked Italian herb sauce that typically incorporates bunches of fresh basil with garlic, pine nuts, olive oil, and Parmesan cheese. Traditional Italian cooks make pesto with a mortar and pestle, but a food processor works just fine.

Shredded Beef Sandwich

SHREDDED BEEF SANDWICHES

1 (3¼-pound) lean boneless chuck roast
⅓ cup white vinegar
½ teaspoon salt
¼ teaspoon ground cloves
⅛ teaspoon garlic powder
1 large onion, cut into 8 wedges
3 bay leaves
9 (1½-ounce) hamburger buns
9 lettuce leaves

Trim fat from roast. Place roast and next 6 ingredients in a slow cooker. Cover and cook at low heat for 11 hours or until roast is tender. Remove roast from slow cooker; let stand 10 minutes. Separate roast into bite-size pieces, and shred meat with 2 forks; set aside.

Strain cooking liquid; discard solids. Cover and freeze at least 1 hour. Skim fat from surface of cooking liquid; discard. Place cooking liquid in a saucepan, and bring to a boil; remove from heat.

Line bottom halves of buns with a lettuce leaf; top each with shredded beef and top half of bun. Serve hot cooking liquid as a dipping sauce. Yield: 9 servings.

PER SERVING: 324 CALORIES (26% FROM FAT)
FAT 9.4G (SATURATED FAT 3.5G)
PROTEIN 32.2G   CARBOHYDRATE 24.5G
CHOLESTEROL 87MG   SODIUM 435MG

GRILLED FLANK STEAK SANDWICH

1 (1½-pound) lean flank steak
½ cup dry white wine
2 tablespoons balsamic vinegar
2 teaspoons coarsely ground pepper
2 teaspoons minced garlic
1 teaspoon dried oregano
Vegetable cooking spray
2 teaspoons olive oil
1 cup thinly sliced green pepper
1 cup thinly sliced sweet red pepper
½ cup thinly sliced onion
½ teaspoon minced garlic
¼ teaspoon sugar
¼ teaspoon salt
8 (2-ounce) French bread rolls, split

Trim fat from steak. Place steak in a large shallow dish. Combine wine and next 4 ingredients; pour over steak. Cover and marinate in refrigerator 8 hours, turning occasionally.

Coat a large nonstick skillet with cooking spray; add oil. Place over medium-high heat until hot. Add peppers, onion, and ½ teaspoon garlic; sauté 4 minutes. Sprinkle with sugar and salt; sauté an additional 2 minutes or until crisp-tender. Remove from heat, and keep warm.

Remove steak from marinade. Place marinade in a small saucepan; bring to a boil. Reduce heat, and simmer 5 minutes.

Coat grill rack with cooking spray; place on grill over medium-hot coals (350° to 400°). Place steak on rack, and grill 6 to 7 minutes on each side or to desired degree of doneness, basting frequently with marinade.

Slice steak diagonally across grain into ¼-inch-thick slices. Place bottom halves of rolls on a serving platter. Divide steak among bottom halves. Spoon pepper mixture evenly over steak. Top with remaining halves of rolls. Yield: 8 servings.

PER SERVING: 344 CALORIES (32% FROM FAT)
FAT 12.1G (SATURATED FAT 4.6G)
PROTEIN 21.8G CARBOHYDRATE 34.5G
CHOLESTEROL 46MG SODIUM 458MG

PHILLY STEAK SANDWICH

Keep the fat low in this Philadelphia classic by using lean sirloin and reduced-fat cheese.

1 pound lean boneless sirloin steak
2 tablespoons Dijon mustard
2 tablespoons dry red wine
1 teaspoon coarsely ground pepper
¼ teaspoon garlic powder
Vegetable cooking spray
1 small onion, thinly sliced and separated into rings
½ cup canned reduced-sodium beef broth, undiluted
1 tablespoon white wine vinegar
¼ teaspoon salt
¼ teaspoon coarsely ground pepper
2 (6-inch) French baguettes, split
2 (1-ounce) slices reduced-fat provolone cheese, divided
2 tablespoons creamy mustard blend, divided

Trim fat from steak; set aside. Combine Dijon mustard and next 3 ingredients; spread on both sides of steak. Place steak on rack of a broiler pan coated with cooking spray. Broil 4 inches from heat (with electric oven door partially opened) 4 to 5 minutes on each side or until a meat thermometer inserted in thickest part of steak registers 150°. Let stand 5 minutes; wrap with plastic wrap, and cool at least 15 minutes. Chill 1 hour.

Sauté onion in a nonstick skillet coated with cooking spray until tender. Add broth and next 3 ingredients; bring to a boil, and cook until liquid evaporates. Set aside.

Cut steak diagonally across grain into thin slices. Place slices evenly on bottom halves of baguettes; top evenly with onion mixture and cheese. Spread baguette tops evenly with creamy mustard blend, and place on sandwiches. Cut in half, and serve immediately, or wrap in plastic wrap, and chill up to 4 hours. Yield: 4 servings.

PER SERVING: 308 CALORIES (28% FROM FAT)
FAT 9.6G (SATURATED FAT 4.0G)
PROTEIN 32.3G CARBOHYDRATE 19.1G
CHOLESTEROL 84MG SODIUM 635MG

ROAST BEEF AND SWISS SANDWICHES

¼ cup commercial oil-free Italian dressing
2 tablespoons water
½ teaspoon beef-flavored bouillon granules
1 small green pepper, seeded and cut into rings
1 small sweet yellow pepper, seeded and cut into rings
1 medium onion, thinly sliced and separated into rings
2 teaspoons cornstarch
½ cup water
2 teaspoons low-sodium Worcestershire sauce
12 (¾-ounce) slices reduced-calorie Italian bread, toasted
¾ pound thinly sliced cooked roast beef
6 tomato slices
6 (½-ounce) slices reduced-fat Swiss cheese

Combine first 3 ingredients in a large nonstick skillet; bring to a boil. Add pepper rings and onion rings. Cover, reduce heat, and simmer 5 minutes or until vegetables are tender, stirring occasionally.

Combine cornstarch, water, and Worcestershire sauce; stir well. Add to pepper mixture; bring to a boil. Cook until thickened, stirring often.

Place 6 bread slices on a large baking sheet, and top bread slices evenly with roast beef. Spoon pepper mixture evenly over beef. Top each sandwich with 1 tomato slice and 1 cheese slice.

Broil 5½ inches from heat (with electric oven door partially opened) 2 to 3 minutes or until cheese melts. Top with remaining bread slices. Serve immediately. Yield: 6 servings.

PER SERVING: 266 CALORIES (21% FROM FAT)
FAT 6.3G (SATURATED FAT 2.7G)
PROTEIN 27.6G   CARBOHYDRATE 26.0G
CHOLESTEROL 56MG   SODIUM 434MG

Roast Beef and Swiss Sandwiches

Beef Fajitas with Chunky Guacamole

BEEF FAJITAS WITH CHUNKY GUACAMOLE

1½ pounds lean boneless round steak
2 tablespoons lime juice
½ teaspoon salt
⅛ teaspoon pepper
4 cloves garlic, minced
½ cup chopped fresh cilantro
½ cup chopped tomato
¼ cup chopped onion
12 (6-inch) flour tortillas
Vegetable cooking spray
1½ cups shredded iceberg lettuce
Chunky Guacamole
¾ cup nonfat sour cream

Partially freeze steak; trim fat from steak. Slice steak diagonally across grain into ¼-inch strips. Combine steak and next 4 ingredients in a shallow dish; cover and marinate steak in refrigerator 6 to 8 hours, stirring occasionally.

Combine cilantro, tomato, and onion in a small bowl; stir well. Cover and chill at least 1 hour.

Wrap tortillas in aluminum foil. Bake at 325° for 15 minutes. Coat a large nonstick skillet with cooking spray; place over medium-high heat until hot. Add steak; cook 5 to 6 minutes or until steak is browned, stirring often. Remove steak from skillet using a slotted spoon, and divide evenly among tortillas; roll up tortillas.

To serve, arrange fajitas on a serving platter; top evenly with lettuce, tomato mixture, and Chunky Guacamole. Top each serving with 1 tablespoon sour cream. Yield: 12 servings.

CHUNKY GUACAMOLE

¼ cup plus 1 tablespoon finely chopped
    tomato
1 tablespoon chopped green onion
½ teaspoon lime juice
⅛ teaspoon salt
½ small jalapeño pepper, seeded and finely
    chopped
1 clove garlic, minced
½ medium avocado, peeled and cut into
    ½-inch cubes

Combine first 6 ingredients in a small bowl; stir well. Add avocado, and toss gently. Serve immediately. Yield: ¾ cup.

PER SERVING: 225 CALORIES (27% FROM FAT)
FAT 6.8G (SATURATED FAT 2.0G)
PROTEIN 16.4G   CARBOHYDRATE 25.8G
CHOLESTEROL 36MG   SODIUM 165MG

SLOPPY JOES

1 pound ground round
¾ cup minced onion
½ cup diced green pepper
¼ cup diced celery
1 clove garlic, minced
½ cup water
½ cup reduced-calorie ketchup
2 tablespoons brown sugar
2 tablespoons tomato paste
1 tablespoon vinegar
¼ teaspoon dry mustard
¼ teaspoon chili powder
¼ teaspoon pepper
6 (1½-ounce) whole wheat hamburger buns

Combine first 5 ingredients in a nonstick skillet. Cook over medium heat until beef is browned, stirring until it crumbles. Drain and pat dry with paper towels. Wipe drippings from skillet with a paper towel.

Return beef mixture to skillet; add water and next 7 ingredients, stirring well. Reduce heat; cook, uncovered, 15 minutes, stirring occasionally.

Spoon ½ cup beef mixture onto bottom half of each bun; cover mixture with top half of bun. Yield: 6 servings.

PER SERVING: 258 CALORIES (26% FROM FAT)
FAT 7.4G (SATURATED FAT 2.4G)
PROTEIN 20.2G   CARBOHYDRATE 26.7G
CHOLESTEROL 59MG   SODIUM 276MG

Triple Treat Burger

Triple Treat Burgers

1 pound ground round
2 tablespoons minced green pepper
1 tablespoon instant minced onion
2 teaspoons low-sodium Worcestershire sauce
¼ teaspoon pepper
1 teaspoon Dijon mustard
2 (¾-ounce) slices low-fat process Swiss
   cheese, quartered
2 (¾-ounce) slices lean cooked ham,
   quartered
Vegetable cooking spray
4 (2-ounce) onion-flavored buns
4 leaf lettuce leaves
4 (¼-inch-thick) tomato slices

Combine first 5 ingredients in a large bowl; stir well. Shape mixture into 8 (5-inch) patties. Spread each of 4 patties with ¼ teaspoon mustard; top each with 2 cheese pieces and 2 ham pieces. Top filled patties with remaining 4 patties, pressing edges to seal.

Coat grill rack with cooking spray; place on grill over medium-hot coals (350° to 400°). Place patties on rack; grill, covered, 5 to 7 minutes on each side or until done. Place 1 cooked patty on bottom half of each bun. Top each patty with 1 lettuce leaf, 1 tomato slice, and top half of bun. Yield: 4 servings.

Per Serving: 380 Calories (25% from Fat)
Fat 10.4g (Saturated Fat 3.4g)
Protein 34.6g   Carbohydrate 35.2g
Cholesterol 77mg   Sodium 563mg

Grilling Tips

To make cleanup easier, first remove the grill rack, and then coat it with cooking spray. (Spraying over lit coals will cause the coals to flame.)

When grilling a large number of kabobs, place them in a hinged wire basket so that they can be turned more easily.

Italian Calzones

1 (1-pound) loaf commercial frozen white
   bread dough
1 pound ground round
½ cup chopped fresh mushrooms
½ cup finely chopped onion
¼ cup chopped green pepper
½ cup evaporated skimmed milk
3 tablespoons fine, dry breadcrumbs
1½ teaspoons dried oregano
¾ to 1 teaspoon fennel seeds, crushed
½ teaspoon crushed red pepper
3 cloves garlic, minced
¾ cup no-salt-added tomato sauce
1 teaspoon sugar
¼ teaspoon salt
Vegetable cooking spray

Thaw dough according to package directions.

Combine ground round and next 9 ingredients in a large skillet; stir well. Cook over medium heat 10 minutes or until meat is browned, stirring until it crumbles. Add tomato sauce, sugar, and salt; cook 6 minutes, stirring occasionally. Remove from heat; let mixture cool slightly.

Divide dough into 8 equal portions. Working with 1 portion at a time (cover remaining portions to keep dough from drying out), roll each portion to ⅛-inch thickness. Place on a large baking sheet coated with cooking spray, and pat each portion into a 6-inch circle with floured fingertips. Spoon ⅓ cup meat mixture onto half of each circle; moisten edges of dough with water. Fold dough over filling; press edges together with a fork to seal. Lightly coat with cooking spray.

Bake at 375° for 20 minutes or until golden. Remove from oven, and lightly coat again with cooking spray. Serve warm. Yield: 8 servings.

Per Serving: 343 Calories (16% from Fat)
Fat 6.1g (Saturated Fat 1.1g)
Protein 22.3g   Carbohydrate 48.9g
Cholesterol 34mg   Sodium 592mg

Italian Meatball Sandwiches

ITALIAN MEATBALL SANDWICHES

6 (2-ounce) whole wheat submarine loaves
1 pound ground round
¼ cup finely chopped onion
3 tablespoons Italian-seasoned breadcrumbs
2 tablespoons water
¼ teaspoon pepper
1 egg white, lightly beaten
Vegetable cooking spray
1½ cups low-fat, reduced-sodium pasta sauce
¾ cup (3 ounces) shredded part-skim
  mozzarella cheese
Fresh basil sprigs (optional)

Slanting knife at an angle, cut an oval piece out of top of each loaf; set loaves aside, reserving top pieces of loaves for another use.

Combine ground round and next 5 ingredients in a bowl; stir well. Shape mixture into 36 (1-inch) balls. Coat a large nonstick skillet with cooking spray; place over medium heat until hot. Add meatballs, and cook 8 to 10 minutes or until browned on all sides, turning frequently. Remove from heat, and pat dry with paper towels. Wipe drippings from skillet with a paper towel.

Return meatballs to skillet; add pasta sauce, and cook over medium-low heat 10 minutes or until thoroughly heated. Set aside, and keep warm.

Place submarine loaves on an ungreased baking

Use a 1-tablespoon ice cream scoop to make just-the-right-size meatballs for this sandwich.

sheet; top each with 6 meatballs. Spoon sauce evenly over meatballs. Sprinkle evenly with mozzarella cheese. Bake at 400° for 5 minutes or until cheese melts. Garnish with basil sprigs, if desired. Yield: 6 servings.

PER SERVING: 269 CALORIES (25% FROM FAT)
FAT 7.6G (SATURATED FAT 2.4G)
PROTEIN 25.8G   CARBOHYDRATE 23.4G
CHOLESTEROL 60MG   SODIUM 621MG

BARBECUED LAMB SANDWICH

3 pounds lean boneless leg of lamb
1½ cups chopped onion
1 cup water
1 clove garlic, minced
½ teaspoon pepper
Dash of hot sauce
1 (6-ounce) can tomato paste
1 (4-ounce) can chopped green chiles,
  undrained
10 (1½-ounce) hamburger buns

Trim fat from lamb. Place lamb and next 3 ingredients in a large Dutch oven. Bring to a simmer; cover and cook over low heat 2 hours or until lamb is tender. Remove lamb from pan, reserving 2 cups liquid. Separate lamb into bite-sized pieces; shred meat with 2 forks.

Combine lamb, reserved cooking liquid, pepper, and next 3 ingredients in pan. Cover and cook over low heat 30 minutes, stirring occasionally. Spoon ½ cup lamb mixture onto bottom halves of buns; top each with top half of bun. Yield: 10 servings.

PER SERVING: 317 CALORIES (26% FROM FAT)
FAT 9.0G (SATURATED FAT 2.4G)
PROTEIN 27.8G   CARBOHYDRATE 30.1G
CHOLESTEROL 87MG   SODIUM 230MG

SAVORY MOCK GYROS

1 pound lean ground lamb
1 teaspoon dried oregano
½ teaspoon dried marjoram
⅛ teaspoon salt
⅛ teaspoon pepper
1 clove garlic, minced
Vegetable cooking spray
2 (8-inch) whole wheat pita bread rounds, cut
   in half crosswise
1 cup finely shredded leaf lettuce
Yogurt-Cucumber Sauce
1 small purple onion, thinly sliced and
   separated into rings
¾ cup chopped tomato

Combine first 6 ingredients in a large bowl; stir well. Shape mixture into 16 (1-inch) meatballs. Place meatballs on rack of a broiler pan coated with cooking spray. Broil 5½ inches from heat (with electric oven door partially opened) 12 to 13 minutes or to desired degree of doneness.

Line each pita half with ¼ cup lettuce; place 4 meatballs in each pita half. Top each serving evenly with Yogurt-Cucumber Sauce, onion, and tomato. Yield: 4 servings.

YOGURT-CUCUMBER SAUCE

½ cup plain nonfat yogurt
⅓ cup finely chopped cucumber
¾ teaspoon dried dillweed
1 clove garlic, minced

Combine all ingredients in a small bowl; stir well. Cover and chill thoroughly. Yield: ⅔ cup.

PER SERVING: 331 CALORIES (26% FROM FAT)
FAT 9.5G (SATURATED FAT 3.0G)
PROTEIN 30.1G   CARBOHYDRATE 27.8G
CHOLESTEROL 81MG   SODIUM 171MG

LAMB POCKETS WITH WHITE BEAN SALSA

¾ pound lean boneless lamb
1 teaspoon ground cumin
1 teaspoon chili powder
¼ teaspoon garlic powder
⅛ teaspoon salt
Vegetable cooking spray
¼ cup plus 2 tablespoons plain nonfat yogurt,
   divided
3 (6-inch) pita bread rounds, cut in half
   crosswise
24 peeled cucumber slices (⅛ inch thick)
White Bean Salsa

Cut lamb into ¼-inch-wide strips. Combine cumin, chili powder, garlic powder, and salt, stirring well. Sprinkle evenly over lamb. Coat a large non-stick skillet with cooking spray; place over high heat until hot. Add lamb, and cook until browned on all sides, stirring often.

Spread 1 tablespoon yogurt in each pita half; place 4 cucumber slices over yogurt in each pita. Spoon lamb mixture evenly into pita halves. Top lamb with White Bean Salsa. Yield: 6 servings.

WHITE BEAN SALSA

½ cup drained canned navy beans
¼ cup seeded, diced tomato
¼ cup diced green pepper
¼ cup minced purple onion
2 tablespoons minced fresh cilantro
1 tablespoon seeded, minced jalapeño pepper
1 tablespoon lime juice
¼ teaspoon ground cumin
¼ teaspoon chili powder

Combine all ingredients in a small bowl, stirring well. Cover and let stand 2 hours. Yield: 1⅓ cups.

PER SERVING: 213 CALORIES (22% FROM FAT)
FAT 5.2G (SATURATED FAT 1.6G)
PROTEIN 17.2G   CARBOHYDRATE 22.7G
CHOLESTEROL 41MG   SODIUM 301MG

HARVEST PORK SANDWICHES

Turn to page 138 if you'd like to make your own chutney, although there are several commercial varieties available.

2 (½-pound) pork tenderloins
2 egg whites, lightly beaten
½ cup toasted wheat germ
Vegetable cooking spray
1 teaspoon vegetable oil
2 (7-ounce) French bread baguettes
¼ cup chutney
¼ cup nonfat mayonnaise
1 apple, cored and thinly sliced
1 small purple onion, thinly sliced

Trim fat from pork. Slice pork diagonally across grain into ½-inch-thick slices. Place pork between 2 sheets of heavy-duty plastic wrap; flatten to ¼-inch thickness, using a meat mallet or rolling pin.

Dip pork slices in egg white, and sprinkle both sides of each slice with wheat germ.

Coat a large nonstick skillet with cooking spray; add oil. Place over medium-high heat until hot. Add pork, and cook 4 minutes on each side or until browned. Drain on paper towels.

Cut each baguette crosswise into quarters to make 8 sandwich rolls. Split each roll in half lengthwise. Divide pork evenly among bottom halves of rolls. Combine chutney and mayonnaise; spread chutney mixture evenly over pork.

Coat a large nonstick skillet with cooking spray; place over medium-high heat until hot. Add apple and onion; sauté until tender. Spoon apple mixture evenly over chutney mixture; place tops of rolls on sandwiches. Yield: 8 servings.

PER SERVING: 282 CALORIES (12% FROM FAT)
FAT 3.8G (SATURATED FAT 1.0G)
PROTEIN 18.4G   CARBOHYDRATE 42.1G
CHOLESTEROL 36MG   SODIUM 441MG

PORK FAJITAS WITH AVOCADO-CORN SALSA

2 (½-pound) pork tenderloins
¾ cup no-salt-added chunky salsa, divided
½ cup light beer
½ cup lime juice, divided
2 teaspoons ground cumin
½ teaspoon garlic powder
1 teaspoon hot sauce
¾ cup frozen whole-kernel corn, thawed
¾ cup peeled, diced avocado
¼ cup finely chopped sweet red pepper
3 tablespoons minced fresh cilantro
¼ teaspoon garlic powder
6 (7-inch) flour tortillas
Vegetable cooking spray
Fresh cilantro sprigs (optional)

Partially freeze pork; trim fat from pork, and cut into ¼-inch-thick slices. Place pork slices in a heavy-duty, zip-top plastic bag. Combine ½ cup salsa, beer, ¼ cup plus 2 tablespoons lime juice, cumin, ½ teaspoon garlic powder, and hot sauce; pour over pork. Seal bag, and shake until pork slices are well coated. Marinate pork slices in refrigerator at least 3 hours, turning bag occasionally.

Combine remaining ¼ cup salsa, remaining 2 tablespoons lime juice, corn, avocado, red pepper, minced cilantro, and ¼ teaspoon garlic powder in a small bowl. Set aside.

Wrap tortillas in heavy-duty aluminum foil. Bake at 350° for 5 minutes or until thoroughly heated. Set aside, and keep warm.

Remove pork from marinade, discarding marinade. Coat a large nonstick skillet with cooking spray; place over medium-high heat until hot. Add pork, and cook 4 minutes or until done, stirring often. Place pork evenly down centers of tortillas. Top each with ¼ cup corn mixture; roll up tortillas. Garnish with fresh cilantro sprigs, if desired. Serve immediately. Yield: 6 servings.

PER SERVING: 275 CALORIES (28% FROM FAT)
FAT 8.7G (SATURATED FAT 1.9G)
PROTEIN 21.7G   CARBOHYDRATE 27.6G
CHOLESTEROL 56MG   SODIUM 252MG

GRILLED PORK WITH SWEET-AND-SOUR RED CABBAGE

½ cup canned no-salt-added beef broth, undiluted
¼ cup unsweetened apple juice
¼ cup chopped onion
1 tablespoon chili powder
2 tablespoons cider vinegar
2 tablespoons low-sodium Worcestershire sauce
2 cloves garlic, chopped
2 (½-pound) pork tenderloins
¼ teaspoon freshly ground pepper
⅛ teaspoon salt
Vegetable cooking spray
2 tablespoons no-salt-added tomato paste
2 (6-ounce) French bread baguettes
Sweet-and-Sour Red Cabbage

Combine first 7 ingredients in a large heavy-duty, zip-top plastic bag; seal bag, and shake well. Trim fat from pork. Add pork to bag; seal bag, and shake until pork is well coated. Marinate in refrigerator 8 hours, turning bag occasionally.

Remove pork from marinade, reserving marinade. Sprinkle pork with pepper and salt. Coat grill rack with cooking spray, and place on grill over medium-hot coals (350° to 400°). Place pork on rack, and insert meat thermometer into thickest part of pork. Grill 25 minutes or until meat thermometer registers 160°, turning frequently. Let pork stand 10 minutes. Slice diagonally across grain into thin slices.

Place reserved marinade in a saucepan; bring to a boil. Reduce heat; simmer 3 minutes. Add tomato paste, stirring with a wire whisk until smooth; cook an additional 3 minutes.

Cut each baguette in half lengthwise; cut each loaf into quarters crosswise to make 8 sandwich rolls. Divide sliced pork evenly among bottom halves of rolls. Spread each with 1½ tablespoons cooked marinade mixture. Spoon Sweet-and-Sour Red Cabbage evenly onto each roll, and place tops of rolls on sandwiches. Yield: 8 servings.

SWEET-AND-SOUR RED CABBAGE

8 cups shredded red cabbage
1 large purple onion, thinly sliced
½ cup water
½ cup red wine vinegar
3 tablespoons sugar
⅛ teaspoon salt
¼ teaspoon freshly ground pepper
Vegetable cooking spray

Combine first 7 ingredients in a large saucepan coated with cooking spray. Cover and cook red cabbage mixture over medium heat 30 minutes or until red cabbage is tender, stirring occasionally. Serve red cabbage mixture warm or chilled. Yield: 3 cups.

PER SERVING: 287 CALORIES (13% FROM FAT)
FAT 4.3G (SATURATED FAT 1.2G)
PROTEIN 19.4G   CARBOHYDRATE 42.6G
CHOLESTEROL 45MG   SODIUM 426MG

FYI

Pork tenderloin is considered by many to be the choice cut of pork for low-fat eating. It is very lean yet naturally tender and can be cooked by either dry- or moist-heat methods. Grilling is an excellent way to prepare the whole tenderloin. When it is done, slice it diagonally into serving portions.

Tenderloin will be tender and juicy when the meat is still slightly pink in the center. If overcooked, it can be tough and dry. For the best results, use a meat thermometer; when it registers 160°, the tenderloin is done.

Grilled Pork with Sweet-and-Sour Red Cabbage

Harvest Stew (recipe on page 119)

SOUP POT SPECIALTIES

*S*imple comfort and satisfaction—that's what you'll experience with homemade soups and stews. Serve the lighter ones, such as Vegetable Beef Soup (page 115), with a sandwich for lunch or supper. Accompany the heartier Beef Taco Soup (page 116) and the stews with only salad or bread on the side. Feel free to adjust the portion sizes, depending on what other foods you plan to serve.

Following the soups are recipes for both a beef and a veal ragout, a Four-Meat Burgoo (page 123) from Kentucky, and several all-American stews. Rounding out the chapter on pages 126 and 127 are three versions of spicy chili, each made with a different meat.

Beef Brown Stock

BEEF BROWN STOCK

*Use this salt-free homemade stock in the Country Beef Ragout recipe on
page 118 or in the place of beef broth for other soups. You can even
substitute it for water when cooking pasta, rice, or grains.*

3 pounds beef shank bones, halved
3 large onions, quartered (about 1¾ pounds)
10 cups water
4 medium carrots, quartered (about ½ pound)
2 tablespoons black peppercorns
3 cloves garlic, crushed
3 bay leaves
1 bunch fresh parsley

Combine beef shanks and onion in an 8-quart
Dutch oven or stockpot; cook over medium-high
heat 20 minutes or until shanks and onion turn very
brown, stirring often. Add water and remaining
ingredients; bring to a boil. Reduce heat, and simmer, uncovered, 2 hours. Remove from heat, and
let cool.

Strain stock through a cheesecloth-lined colander
into a bowl; discard solids. Cover and chill at least
24 hours. Skim solidified fat from surface, and discard. Yield: 7 (1-cup) servings.

PER SERVING: 22 CALORIES (0% FROM FAT)
FAT 0.0G (SATURATED FAT 0.0G)
PROTEIN 0.5G   CARBOHYDRATE 1.9G
CHOLESTEROL 0MG   SODIUM 7MG

To make Beef Brown Stock, combine water, vegetables, and seasonings in a large Dutch oven, and simmer 2 hours.

Strain stock through a cheesecloth-lined colander into a bowl; discard solids.

Cover and chill the stock at least 24 hours; skim solidified fat from surface.

MEATBALL SOUP

1 pound ground round
¾ cup soft breadcrumbs
2 tablespoons skim milk
¼ teaspoon caraway seeds
1 egg white
Vegetable cooking spray
2¼ cups water
2 cups sliced fresh mushrooms
1 cup thinly sliced carrot
½ cup chopped celery
½ cup chopped onion
2 tablespoons chopped fresh parsley
2 tablespoons red wine vinegar
¼ teaspoon caraway seeds
⅛ teaspoon pepper
2 cloves garlic, minced
1 (10½-ounce) can beef broth
2 cups loosely packed torn fresh spinach

Combine first 5 ingredients in a bowl; stir well. Shape into 24 (1½-inch) meatballs; set aside.

Coat a large nonstick skillet with cooking spray; place over medium heat until hot. Add meatballs; cook 10 minutes or until done, turning occasionally. Drain and pat dry with paper towels.

Combine water and next 10 ingredients in a large saucepan; bring to a boil. Cover, reduce heat, and simmer 15 minutes or until vegetables are tender.

Stir in meatballs and spinach, and cook an additional 3 minutes or until thoroughly heated. Yield: 7 (1-cup) servings.

PER SERVING: 147 CALORIES (27% FROM FAT)
FAT 4.4G (SATURATED FAT 1.5G)
PROTEIN 18.0G   CARBOHYDRATE 8.7G
CHOLESTEROL 48MG   SODIUM 370MG

Quick Tip

Once you've made a pot of Beef Brown Stock, you can keep it up to three days in the refrigerator or up to three months in the freezer. Ice-cube trays offer a convenient way to freeze the stock.

Each cube is equivalent to about 2 tablespoons. When the stock is frozen, transfer the cubes to zip-top freezer bags. Then pull out the cubes to use in soups or stews as needed.

Vegetable Beef Soup

VEGETABLE BEEF SOUP

This recipe makes enough for two meals. Measure out the needed portions, and freeze the rest of the soup (up to 2 months) to serve another time.

Vegetable cooking spray
½ pound ground chuck
2⅓ cups chopped cabbage
2 cups chopped celery
1⅓ cups sliced carrot
1 cup chopped onion
½ cup chopped green pepper
4 cups canned no-salt-added beef broth, undiluted
2 (14½-ounce) cans no-salt-added whole tomatoes, undrained and chopped
1 (11-ounce) can no-salt-added whole kernel corn, drained
1 teaspoon dried oregano
½ teaspoon dried thyme
½ teaspoon pepper
¼ teaspoon salt

Coat a Dutch oven with cooking spray; place over medium-high heat until hot. Add ground chuck; cook until meat is browned, stirring until it crumbles. Remove meat; drain and pat dry with paper towels. Wipe drippings from Dutch oven with a paper towel.

Coat Dutch oven with cooking spray; place over medium-high heat until hot. Add cabbage, celery, carrot, onion, and green pepper; sauté 5 minutes or until tender.

Return meat to Dutch oven. Add broth and remaining ingredients. Bring to a boil; cover, reduce heat, and simmer 20 to 25 minutes or until vegetables are tender. Yield: 10 (1-cup) servings.

PER SERVING: 112 CALORIES (29% FROM FAT)
FAT 3.6G (SATURATED FAT 1.3G)
PROTEIN 6.2G   CARBOHYDRATE 13.4G
CHOLESTEROL 13MG   SODIUM 117MG

BEEF-MUSHROOM SOUP

Vegetable cooking spray
1 pound ground round
¾ cup chopped onion
¾ cup chopped celery
¾ cup sliced carrot
3 cloves garlic, minced
6 cups sliced fresh mushrooms
3 tablespoons all-purpose flour
4¼ cups canned no-salt-added beef broth, undiluted and divided
¾ teaspoon salt
½ teaspoon dried thyme
½ teaspoon dried marjoram
½ cup cooked long-grain rice (cooked without salt or fat)
⅓ cup skim milk
1½ tablespoons diced pimiento
1½ tablespoons dry sherry

Coat a large Dutch oven with cooking spray; place over medium heat until hot. Add ground round, onion, celery, carrot, and garlic; cook until beef is browned, stirring until it crumbles. Drain beef mixture; pat dry with paper towels. Wipe drippings from Dutch oven with a paper towel. Return mixture to Dutch oven; add mushrooms. Cook 4 minutes or until vegetables are tender, stirring often.

Combine flour and ½ cup broth; stir until smooth. Add flour mixture, remaining 3¾ cups broth, salt, thyme, and marjoram to beef mixture; stir well. Cook, uncovered, over medium heat 30 minutes, stirring occasionally. Stir in rice, milk, pimiento, and sherry; cook just until mixture is thoroughly heated (do not boil). Yield: 8 (1-cup) servings.

PER SERVING: 149 CALORIES (27% FROM FAT)
FAT 4.5G (SATURATED FAT 1.5G)
PROTEIN 14.4G   CARBOHYDRATE 12.0G
CHOLESTEROL 31MG   SODIUM 339MG

BEEF TACO SOUP

3 (6-inch) corn tortillas
Vegetable cooking spray
1 pound ground round
1 cup chopped onion
2 cloves garlic, minced
2 teaspoons chili powder
1 teaspoon ground cumin
¾ teaspoon dried oregano
¾ teaspoon salt
¼ teaspoon pepper
1 (14½-ounce) can no-salt-added whole
    tomatoes, undrained and chopped
1 (16-ounce) can dark red kidney beans,
    drained
1 (13¾-ounce) can no-salt-added beef broth
1 (8-ounce) can no-salt-added tomato sauce
1 (4-ounce) can chopped green chiles
1½ tablespoons seeded, minced jalapeño
    pepper
½ cup finely shredded iceberg lettuce
½ cup chopped tomato
½ cup (2 ounces) shredded reduced-fat sharp
    Cheddar cheese

Cut tortillas into ½-inch-wide strips; cut strips in half crosswise. Place tortilla strips on an ungreased baking sheet. Bake at 350° for 12 to 15 minutes or until crisp. Set aside.

Coat a Dutch oven with cooking spray; place over medium heat until hot. Add ground round, onion, and garlic; cook until beef is browned, stirring until it crumbles. Drain beef mixture; pat dry with paper towels. Wipe drippings from Dutch oven with a paper towel.

Return beef mixture to Dutch oven; add chili powder, cumin, oregano, salt, and pepper, stirring well. Stir in canned tomatoes and next 5 ingredients. Bring to a boil; cover, reduce heat, and simmer 30 minutes, stirring occasionally.

Ladle soup into individual bowls; top evenly with lettuce, ½ cup tomato, cheese, and tortilla strips. Yield: 8 (1-cup) servings.

PER SERVING: 200 CALORIES (23% FROM FAT)
FAT 5.2G (SATURATED FAT 2.0G)
PROTEIN 17.9G   CARBOHYDRATE 20.5G
CHOLESTEROL 36MG   SODIUM 400MG

BEEF AND BARLEY STEW

Barley is a hardy grain used throughout history in soups, breads, and cereals. Pearl barley, a staple in soups and stews, has had the bran removed and has been steamed and polished.

1 pound lean boneless top round steak (½ inch
    thick)
Vegetable cooking spray
1 cup chopped onion
1 cup sliced celery
1 cup sliced carrot
2 cloves garlic, minced
3 cups water
1½ cups no-salt-added tomato juice
¼ cup pearl barley, uncooked
1 tablespoon low-sodium Worcestershire sauce
2 teaspoons beef-flavored bouillon granules
1 teaspoon paprika
½ teaspoon dried marjoram
¼ teaspoon pepper
1 cup frozen English peas, thawed
1 cup sliced fresh mushrooms

Trim fat from steak; cut steak into ½-inch cubes. Coat a Dutch oven with cooking spray; place over medium-high heat until hot. Add steak; cook until browned on all sides, stirring often. Drain and pat dry with paper towels. Wipe drippings from pan with a paper towel.

Coat pan with cooking spray; place over medium-high heat until hot. Add onion, celery, carrot, and garlic; sauté until tender. Add steak, 3 cups water, and next 7 ingredients; stir well. Bring to a boil; cover, reduce heat, and simmer 1½ hours. Add peas and sliced mushrooms; cover and cook an additional 15 minutes or until vegetables are tender. Yield: 7 (1-cup) servings.

PER SERVING: 187 CALORIES (19% FROM FAT)
FAT 3.9G (SATURATED FAT 1.1G)
PROTEIN 19.4G   CARBOHYDRATE 18.5G
CHOLESTEROL 42MG   SODIUM 363MG

CHUNKY BEEF STEW

2 pounds lean boneless top round steak
3 tablespoons all-purpose flour
Vegetable cooking spray
1½ cups coarsely chopped onion
½ teaspoon rubbed sage
¼ teaspoon dried thyme
2 bay leaves
2 cups water
2 teaspoons beef-flavored bouillon granules
¼ teaspoon salt
⅛ teaspoon pepper
1 pound unpeeled round red potatoes, cut into
   1-inch pieces
4 large stalks celery, cut into 1-inch pieces
3 medium carrots, cut into 1-inch pieces

Trim fat from steak. Cut steak into 1-inch cubes; toss with flour. Coat a Dutch oven with cooking spray; place over medium heat until hot. Add steak; cook 6 minutes or until steak loses its pink color, stirring often. Add onion and next 3 ingredients; cook 5 minutes or until onion is tender, stirring often.

Add water, bouillon granules, salt, and pepper; stir well. Bring to a boil; cover, reduce heat, and simmer 45 minutes. Add remaining ingredients, and simmer an additional 45 minutes or until vegetables are tender. Remove and discard bay leaves. Yield: 6 (1⅓-cup) servings.

PER SERVING: 317 CALORIES (19% FROM FAT)
FAT 6.7G (SATURATED FAT 2.4G)
PROTEIN 37.5G   CARBOHYDRATE 25.0G
CHOLESTEROL 86MG   SODIUM 533MG

Chunky Beef Stew

Country Beef Ragout

COUNTRY BEEF RAGOUT

1½ pounds lean boneless round steak
2 tablespoons all-purpose flour
¼ teaspoon salt
½ teaspoon pepper, divided
Vegetable cooking spray
1 teaspoon vegetable oil
1½ cups chopped onion
1½ cups Beef Brown Stock (page 112)
1 cup prune juice
½ teaspoon dried thyme
2 cups peeled, chopped round red potato
1 cup sliced carrot
2 tablespoons lemon juice

Trim fat from steak. Cut steak into ¾-inch cubes. Combine flour, salt, and ¼ teaspoon pepper in a large heavy-duty, zip-top plastic bag. Add steak, shaking well to coat; set aside.

Coat a large Dutch oven with cooking spray; add oil, and place over medium-high heat until hot. Add steak; cook 4 minutes or until browned, stirring often. Add onion; cook 3 minutes. Add remaining ¼ teaspoon pepper, 1½ cups Beef Brown Stock, prune juice, and thyme; bring to a boil. Cover, reduce heat, and simmer 30 minutes. Add potato, carrot, and lemon juice; cover and cook 1 hour or until vegetables are tender, stirring occasionally. Yield: 4 (1½-cup) servings.

PER SERVING: 406 CALORIES (19% FROM FAT)
FAT 8.4G (SATURATED FAT 2.8G)
PROTEIN 42.4G   CARBOHYDRATE 37.6G
CHOLESTEROL 97MG   SODIUM 257MG

HARVEST STEW

(pictured on page 110)

Vegetable cooking spray
1 pound ultra-lean ground beef
¾ cup chopped onion
½ teaspoon pepper
2 cloves garlic, minced
3½ cups water
1 (14½-ounce) can no-salt-added tomatoes, undrained and chopped
2¼ cups peeled, chopped sweet potato
1 cup coarsely chopped unpeeled round red potato
1 cup peeled, chopped acorn squash
2 teaspoons beef-flavored bouillon granules
½ teaspoon chili powder
¼ teaspoon ground allspice
¼ teaspoon ground cloves
2 bay leaves

Coat a Dutch oven with cooking spray; place over medium-high heat until hot. Add ground beef and next 3 ingredients. Cook until beef is browned, stirring until it crumbles. Drain and pat dry with paper towels. Wipe drippings from Dutch oven with a paper towel.

Combine beef mixture, water, and remaining ingredients in Dutch oven; bring to a boil. Cover, reduce heat, and simmer 30 minutes or until vegetables are tender. Remove and discard bay leaves. Yield: 8 (1¼-cup) servings.

PER SERVING: 156 CALORIES (23% FROM FAT)
FAT 3.9G (SATURATED FAT 1.4G)
PROTEIN 12.4G   CARBOHYDRATE 19.6G
CHOLESTEROL 36MG   SODIUM 163MG

OVEN-BAKED BEEF STEW

1½ pounds lean boneless round steak
Vegetable cooking spray
¼ cup all-purpose flour
¾ cup canned no-salt-added beef broth, undiluted
1 (12-ounce) can light beer
2 tablespoons prepared mustard
1 teaspoon sugar
½ teaspoon pepper
¼ teaspoon salt
1½ teaspoons low-sodium Worcestershire sauce
3 cups peeled, diced baking potato
2 cups sliced fresh mushrooms
2 medium carrots, scraped and cut into very thin strips
¾ cup frozen pearl onions
¾ cup frozen English peas

Trim fat from steak; cut steak into 1-inch pieces. Place steak in a 3-quart baking dish or Dutch oven coated with cooking spray.

Combine flour and broth in a medium bowl; stir until smooth. Add beer and next 5 ingredients to flour mixture; stir well. Pour flour mixture over steak, stirring gently to combine. Cover and bake at 350° for 1 hour, stirring occasionally.

Add potato, mushrooms, carrot, and onions to steak mixture, stirring well. Cover and bake 50 minutes. Stir in peas; cover and bake an additional 10 minutes or until steak and vegetables are tender. Yield: 6 (1½-cup) servings.

PER SERVING: 310 CALORIES (18% FROM FAT)
FAT 6.1G (SATURATED FAT 2.0G)
PROTEIN 28.9G   CARBOHYDRATE 30.5G
CHOLESTEROL 63MG   SODIUM 274MG

Health Watch

Many of these stews are loaded with vegetables and starchy foods, like potatoes, rice, and pasta. That's good news because health experts tell us to eat at least six servings of bread, cereal, rice, or pasta and at least five servings of fruits and vegetables each day.

ORIENTAL BEEF-VEGETABLE STEW

1 pound lean boneless top round steak
    (½ inch thick)
Vegetable cooking spray
1 medium onion, sliced
2 cloves garlic, minced
1 (14½-ounce) can no-salt-added whole
    tomatoes, undrained and chopped
2½ cups water
2 tablespoons low-sodium soy sauce
1 tablespoon brown sugar
2 teaspoons peeled, grated gingerroot
1½ cups sliced carrot
1 cup sliced fresh mushrooms
½ cup fresh bean sprouts
1 (4-ounce) jar sliced pimiento, drained
1½ cups broccoli flowerets

Trim fat from steak; cut steak into 1-inch pieces. Coat a Dutch oven with cooking spray; place over medium-high heat until hot. Add steak; cook until browned on all sides, stirring often. Drain and pat dry with paper towels. Wipe drippings from Dutch oven with a paper towel.

Coat Dutch oven with cooking spray; place over medium-high heat until hot. Add onion and garlic; sauté until onion is tender.

Add steak, tomato, water, soy sauce, brown sugar, and gingerroot, stirring well. Bring to a boil; cover, reduce heat, and simmer 1½ hours.

Add carrot; cover and cook 20 minutes. Stir in mushrooms, bean sprouts, and pimiento; cover and cook 15 minutes. Add broccoli, and cook an additional 15 minutes or until meat and broccoli are tender. Yield: 7 (1-cup) servings.

PER SERVING: 141 CALORIES (20% FROM FAT)
FAT 3.1G (SATURATED FAT 1.0G)
PROTEIN 17.2G   CARBOHYDRATE 11.7G
CHOLESTEROL 37MG   SODIUM 199MG

VEAL RAGOUT

Ragout, derived from the French word ragoûter meaning "to revive the appetite," is a well-seasoned mixture of meat and vegetables cooked in a thick sauce.

1½ pounds lean boneless veal
¼ cup plus 3 tablespoons all-purpose flour
½ teaspoon pepper
Vegetable cooking spray
1 tablespoon vegetable oil
3 cups water
1 (13¾-ounce) can no-salt-added beef broth
¼ cup tomato puree
1 teaspoon dried thyme
1 teaspoon dried parsley flakes
½ teaspoon salt
1 clove garlic, crushed
1 small bay leaf
4 cups peeled, cubed red potato
4 carrots, scraped and cut into 1-inch pieces
1 cup frozen English peas

Trim fat from veal; cut veal into 1-inch pieces. Combine flour and pepper; dredge veal in flour mixture. Reserve remaining flour mixture. Coat a large Dutch oven with cooking spray; add oil. Place over medium-high heat until hot. Add veal; cook until browned on all sides, stirring often. Drain and pat dry with paper towels. Wipe drippings from Dutch oven with a paper towel.

Return veal to Dutch oven. Combine reserved flour mixture, water, and next 6 ingredients, stirring well. Add flour mixture and bay leaf to veal. Bring to a boil; cover, reduce heat, and simmer 1 hour. Add potato and carrot; cover and simmer 45 minutes or until veal is tender. Stir in peas; cover and cook 10 minutes or until peas are tender. Remove and discard bay leaf. Yield: 9 (1-cup) servings.

PER SERVING: 200 CALORIES (14% FROM FAT)
FAT 3.1G (SATURATED FAT 0.7G)
PROTEIN 18.5G   CARBOHYDRATE 23.7G
CHOLESTEROL 55MG   SODIUM 238MG

Veal Ragout

Veal Stew with White Polenta

VEAL STEW WITH WHITE POLENTA

*You can make this hearty stew with beef instead of veal, if desired; just substitute 2
pounds of lean boneless bottom round roast for the veal.*

2 pounds lean veal stew meat
2 tablespoons olive oil
3 cloves garlic, minced
2 cups (¾-inch) sliced carrot
1½ cups frozen pearl onions
¼ cup chopped fresh flat-leaf parsley
½ teaspoon dried basil
¼ teaspoon salt
¼ teaspoon pepper
2 cups dry red wine

1 cup canned crushed tomatoes
1 (10½-ounce) can low-sodium
    chicken broth
2 bay leaves
4 cups halved fresh mushrooms
2 teaspoons cornstarch
1 teaspoon water
White Polenta
3 tablespoons grated Parmesan cheese
Flat-leaf parsley (optional)

Trim fat from veal. Cut veal into 1½-inch cubes. Heat oil in a large Dutch oven over medium-high heat. Add veal and garlic; cook 5 minutes or until veal loses its pink color. Add carrot and next 9 ingredients; bring to a boil. Cover, reduce heat, and simmer 1 hour and 15 minutes.

Add mushrooms, and cook, uncovered, 45 minutes or until veal is tender. Combine cornstarch and water; add to stew. Cook, stirring constantly, 2 minutes or until slightly thickened. Remove and discard bay leaves. Ladle ½ cup White Polenta into each of 9 individual pasta bowls; top each with 1 cup stew and 1 teaspoon Parmesan cheese. Garnish with parsley, if desired. Yield: 9 servings.

WHITE POLENTA
1½ cups white cornmeal
¾ teaspoon salt
5 cups water
1 clove garlic, crushed

Combine cornmeal and salt in a large saucepan. Gradually add water and garlic, stirring constantly with a wire whisk. Bring to a boil; reduce heat to medium-low. Cook, uncovered, 15 minutes or until thickened, stirring often. Serve warm. Yield: 9 (½-cup) servings.

PER SERVING: 304 CALORIES (18% FROM FAT)
FAT 6.1G (SATURATED FAT 1.4G)
PROTEIN 26.0G CARBOHYDRATE 27.1G
CHOLESTEROL 80MG SODIUM 419MG

Fat Alert

To keep soups and stews virtually free of fat, start with fat-free broth or stock (see Beef Brown Stock on page 112). If you don't have time to prepare it yourself, canned broth works nicely. But be aware that some brands of canned broth contain fat. To defat commercial broth, place the unopened can in the refrigerator an hour or so before using. When you open the can, skim off the layer of solidified fat.

FOUR-MEAT BURGOO

Burgoo is a stew of Southern origin, featuring at least two kinds of meat and a garden's worth of vegetables.

¼ pound lean boneless round steak
¼ pound veal cutlets
¼ pound lean boneless pork shoulder
4 (6-ounce) skinned chicken breast halves
1½ quarts water
1 (14½-ounce) can no-salt-added whole tomatoes, undrained and chopped
1 (8¾-ounce) can no-salt-added whole kernel corn, drained
1 cup chopped onion
¾ cup shredded cabbage
¾ cup thinly sliced okra
½ cup peeled, cubed small round red potato
½ cup frozen lima beans
½ cup chopped green pepper
⅓ cup sliced carrot
¼ cup chopped fresh parsley
2 hot red peppers
2½ teaspoons low-sodium Worcestershire sauce
¼ teaspoon salt
⅛ teaspoon ground red pepper

Trim fat from steak, veal, and pork; cut into 1-inch pieces. Combine steak, veal, pork, chicken, and water in a Dutch oven; bring to a boil. Cover, reduce heat, and simmer 30 minutes or until tender.

Remove meat and chicken from broth; reserving broth. Let chicken cool to touch. Bone chicken, and cut into bite-size pieces. Skim and discard fat from reserved broth.

Combine meat, chicken, reserved broth, tomato, and remaining ingredients in Dutch oven, stirring well; bring to a boil. Reduce heat, and simmer, uncovered, 2 to 2½ hours or until mixture is thickened, stirring occasionally. Remove and discard hot red peppers. Yield: 8 (1-cup) servings.

PER SERVING: 228 CALORIES (21% FROM FAT)
FAT 5.2G (SATURATED FAT 1.6G)
PROTEIN 26.7G CARBOHYDRATE 15.8G
CHOLESTEROL 72MG SODIUM 172MG

Lamb Stew

LAMB STEW

¾ pound lean boneless leg of lamb
½ cup all-purpose flour
Vegetable cooking spray
4 cups water, divided
1 tablespoon dried Italian seasoning
½ teaspoon salt
⅛ to ¼ teaspoon pepper
4 bay leaves
1 clove garlic, minced
3 medium round red potatoes, peeled and each
     cut into 8 wedges (about ¾ pound)
1½ cups (½-inch) sliced carrot
1 cup coarsely chopped onion

Trim fat from lamb, and cut lamb into 1-inch cubes. Combine lamb and flour in a large heavy-duty, zip-top plastic bag, shaking to coat.

Coat an ovenproof Dutch oven with cooking spray; place over medium heat until hot. Remove lamb from bag, reserving remaining flour. Add lamb to Dutch oven, and cook, stirring constantly, until browned. Remove from Dutch oven; set aside.

Place reserved flour in a bowl. Gradually add 1 cup water, blending with a wire whisk; add to Dutch oven. Stir in remaining 3 cups water, Italian seasoning, and next 4 ingredients; bring to a boil. Add lamb, potato, carrot, and onion; stir well.

Cover and bake at 350° for 1 hour and 15 minutes or until lamb is tender, stirring once. Remove and discard bay leaves. Yield: 4 (1½-cup) servings.

PER SERVING: 290 CALORIES (14% FROM FAT)
FAT 4.6G (SATURATED FAT 1.5G)
PROTEIN 22.4G   CARBOHYDRATE 40.1G
CHOLESTEROL 54MG   SODIUM 369MG

ZESTY PORK STEW

Toasting the cumin seeds intensifies their hearty, nutlike flavor.

2 pounds lean boneless pork loin
Olive-oil flavored vegetable cooking spray
1 (14½-ounce) can no-salt-added stewed
    tomatoes, undrained and chopped
1½ cups water
3 cups peeled, cubed red potato
2 cups thinly sliced onion
2 cups sliced carrot
1 teaspoon dried crushed red pepper
1 teaspoon dried oregano
1 teaspoon cumin seeds, toasted
¼ teaspoon salt

   Trim fat from pork; cut pork into 1-inch cubes. Coat a large Dutch oven with cooking spray; place over medium heat until hot. Add pork, and cook until browned on all sides, stirring often. Drain and pat dry with paper towels. Wipe drippings from Dutch oven with a paper towel.
   Return pork to Dutch oven; stir in tomato and water. Bring to a boil; cover, reduce heat, and simmer 45 minutes. Add potato and remaining ingredients; cover and cook 30 minutes. Uncover and cook an additional 25 minutes or until vegetables are tender. Yield: 8 (1-cup) servings.

PER SERVING: 262 CALORIES (31% FROM FAT)
FAT 8.9G (SATURATED FAT 3.0G)
PROTEIN 25.9G   CARBOHYDRATE 19.3G
CHOLESTEROL 68MG   SODIUM 172MG

FYJ

   Many soups, stews, and chilis taste even better when refrigerated a day or so. Many also freeze well. Use airtight plastic freezer containers or zip-top freezer bags, and date each bag. Use the frozen soup within three or four months for optimum flavor.

PORK SUCCOTASH

Lima beans, corn, and sweet red pepper make this dish reminiscent of a true succotash. For a quick, complete meal, add cornbread and a tossed salad.

1 pound lean boneless pork loin
Vegetable cooking spray
1 cup chopped onion
3 cups water
1 (10-ounce) package frozen baby lima beans
1 (10-ounce) package frozen whole kernel
    corn
1 (4-ounce) can chopped green chiles
1 medium-size sweet red pepper, seeded and
    chopped
2 teaspoons chicken-flavored bouillon
    granules
¼ teaspoon salt
⅛ teaspoon pepper
⅛ teaspoon paprika

   Trim fat from pork; cut pork into ½-inch cubes. Coat a Dutch oven with cooking spray; place over medium-high heat until hot. Add pork cubes and onion; cook until pork is browned and onion is tender, stirring often. Drain pork mixture, and pat dry with paper towels. Wipe drippings from Dutch oven with a paper towel.
   Return pork mixture to Dutch oven; add water and remaining ingredients. Bring to a boil; cover, reduce heat, and simmer 20 to 30 minutes or until pork and vegetables are tender. Yield: 7 (1-cup) servings.

PER SERVING: 224 CALORIES (31% FROM FAT)
FAT 7.6G (SATURATED FAT 2.5G)
PROTEIN 18.4G   CARBOHYDRATE 21.3G
CHOLESTEROL 46MG   SODIUM 244MG

PORK CHILI

*Green peppers can be substituted for the poblanos
with some change in taste.*

6 fresh poblano peppers (about ¾ pound)
1¼ pounds fresh ripe tomatillos (about 23
    small)
1½ pounds pork butt steaks
Vegetable cooking spray
1½ cups chopped onion
3 cloves garlic, minced
2 teaspoons ground cumin
1 teaspoon dried oregano
½ teaspoon salt
½ cup chopped fresh cilantro
1 tablespoon lemon juice
4 (6-inch) flour tortillas
¼ cup plain nonfat yogurt
Lemon rind strips (optional)

Cut peppers in half lengthwise; discard seeds and membranes. Place peppers, skin side up, on a foil-lined baking sheet; flatten with palm of hand. Broil peppers 3 inches from heat (with electric oven door partially opened) 10 minutes or until blackened and charred. Place peppers in ice water, and chill 5 minutes. Drain; peel and discard skins. Cut lengthwise into ¼-inch-wide strips, and set aside.

Place tomatillos in a saucepan; add water to cover. Bring to a boil; cook 8 minutes or until tender. Drain tomatillos, reserving 1 cup cooking liquid. Set aside.

Trim fat from pork. Cut pork into 1-inch cubes. Coat a Dutch oven with cooking spray; place over medium-high heat until hot. Add pork; cook 5 minutes or until pork loses its pink color, stirring often. Remove pork from Dutch oven, and drain on paper towels.

Recoat Dutch oven with cooking spray, and place over medium heat. Add pepper strips, onion, and garlic; cook 5 minutes, stirring often. Return pork to Dutch oven . Add tomatillos, reserved 1 cup cooking liquid, cumin, oregano, and salt; stir well. Bring to a boil. Cover, reduce heat, and simmer 1 hour and 45 minutes, stirring occasionally. Stir in cilantro and lemon juice. Cook 5 minutes.

Wrap tortillas in damp paper towels and then in aluminum foil. Bake at 350° for 10 minutes or until softened.

Ladle chili into individual soup bowls; top with yogurt, and garnish with lemon rind, if desired. Serve with warm tortillas. Yield: 4 (1-cup) servings.

PER SERVING: 398 CALORIES (29% FROM FAT)
FAT 13.0G (SATURATED FAT 4.0G)
PROTEIN 30.2G   CARBOHYDRATE 42.2G
CHOLESTEROL 76MG   SODIUM 589MG

CHILE CON CARNE

2¼ pounds lean boneless round steak
Vegetable cooking spray
2 cups chopped onion
4 cloves garlic, minced
2 (14½-ounce) cans no-salt-added whole
    tomatoes, undrained and chopped
2½ cups water
1½ tablespoons ground cumin
¾ teaspoon dried crushed red pepper
½ teaspoon dried oregano
¼ teaspoon salt
1 bay leaf

Trim fat from steak; cut steak into 1-inch pieces. Coat a large Dutch oven with cooking spray; place over medium-high heat until hot. Add steak; cook until browned on all sides, stirring often. Drain well, and pat dry with paper towels. Wipe drippings from Dutch oven with a paper towel.

Coat Dutch oven with cooking spray; place over medium-high heat until hot. Add onion and garlic; sauté 4 to 5 minutes or until tender.

Stir in steak, tomato, and remaining ingredients; bring to a boil. Reduce heat, and simmer, uncovered, 1 hour and 15 minutes or until meat is tender and mixture is thickened, stirring occasionally. Remove and discard bay leaf before serving. Yield: 7 (1-cup) servings.

PER SERVING: 211 CALORIES (31% FROM FAT)
FAT 7.3G (SATURATED FAT 2.5G)
PROTEIN 26.0G   CARBOHYDRATE 9.9G
CHOLESTEROL 70MG   SODIUM 158MG

Spicy Lamb-and-Black Bean Chili

SPICY LAMB-AND-BLACK BEAN CHILI

Vegetable cooking spray
1 pound lean ground lamb
½ cup frozen chopped onion
1½ tablespoons chili powder
2 teaspoons ground cumin
¼ teaspoon salt
¼ to ½ teaspoon ground red pepper
3 (8-ounce) cans no-salt-added tomato sauce
2 (15-ounce) cans black beans, drained
1 (14½-ounce) can no-salt-added whole tomatoes, undrained and chopped
1 (13¾-ounce) can no-salt-added chicken broth
2 (4-ounce) cans chopped green chiles, undrained

Coat a large Dutch oven with cooking spray; place over medium-high heat until hot. Add lamb and chopped onion; cook until meat is browned, stirring until it crumbles. Drain well; wipe drippings from pan with a paper towel. Return lamb mixture to Dutch oven.

Add chili powder and remaining ingredients, and bring to a boil. Reduce heat, and simmer, uncovered, 15 minutes, stirring occasionally. Yield: 7 (1½-cup) servings.

PER SERVING: 278 CALORIES (19% FROM FAT)
FAT 5.8G (SATURATED FAT 1.9G)
PROTEIN 23.5G   CARBOHYDRATE 32.9G
CHOLESTEROL 46MG   SODIUM 421MG

Tomatillo Salsa (recipe on page 137)

SAUCES & CONDIMENTS

A basic white sauce may seem quite bland, but when it is "doctored up" with sherry and mushrooms, it takes on a different character. Sherried Mushroom Sauce (page 132) can transform a simple steak into an elegant entrée fit for company. For more casual meals, top your meat entrée with salsa. And that doesn't mean just a jar of Mexican-seasoned tomato dip. Look to pages 134 through 137 for salsas that go with beef, lamb, and pork.

With this assortment of savory sauces and condiments, you can add richness and flavor to meats without extra fat.

SHERRIED BEEF MARINADE

If the marinade has been used on uncooked meat or poultry, bring the marinade to a full rolling boil before serving it as a sauce over cooked meat.

¼ cup low-sodium Worcestershire sauce
3 tablespoons dry sherry
2 tablespoons water
2 tablespoons lemon juice
1½ tablespoons low-sodium soy sauce
1½ teaspoons dry mustard
1 teaspoon pepper
½ teaspoon minced fresh parsley
1 clove garlic, minced

Combine all ingredients in a small bowl; stir well. Use to marinate beef or veal before cooking. Baste meat with remaining unused marinade while cooking. Yield: ¾ cup.

PER TABLESPOON: 8 CALORIES (11% FROM FAT)
FAT 0.1G (SATURATED FAT 0.0G)
PROTEIN 0.2G CARBOHYDRATE 1.8G
CHOLESTEROL 0MG SODIUM 80MG

CHILI SEASONING

Try this seasoning blend as a lower-sodium alternative to packaged chili seasoning. It contains about 86 percent less sodium than do commercial varieties.

¼ cup chili powder
2 tablespoons plus 2 teaspoons onion powder
1 tablespoon plus 1 teaspoon sugar
1 tablespoon plus 1 teaspoon garlic powder
1 tablespoon plus 1 teaspoon dry mustard
1 tablespoon plus 1 teaspoon ground cumin
1 tablespoon plus 1 teaspoon paprika
1 tablespoon plus 1 teaspoon ground oregano
¼ teaspoon salt

Combine all ingredients in an airtight container. Cover and store at room temperature.

Use to season ground beef or ground turkey for use in chili or tacos. Yield: ¾ cup plus 2 tablespoons.
Note: To make seasoned beef or turkey, brown ¼ pound lean ground beef or turkey in a skillet; drain and pat dry with paper towels. Return beef or turkey to skillet; add 1 tablespoon Chili Seasoning and 2 tablespoons water. Bring to a boil; cover, reduce heat, and simmer 5 minutes.

PER TABLESPOON: 24 CALORIES (30% FROM FAT)
FAT 0.8G (SATURATED FAT 0.1G)
PROTEIN 0.9G CARBOHYDRATE 4.5G
CHOLESTEROL 0MG SODIUM 64MG

CHUNKY SOUTHWESTERN CHILI SAUCE

1 (8-ounce) can no-salt-added tomato sauce
½ cup chopped sweet red pepper
½ cup chopped onion
¼ cup chopped fresh cilantro
2 tablespoons brown sugar
2 tablespoons cider vinegar
2 tablespoons golden tequila
1 teaspoon ground cumin
1 teaspoon chili powder
2 teaspoons seeded, chopped jalapeño pepper
½ teaspoon ground cinnamon
¼ teaspoon garlic powder
¼ teaspoon ground red pepper
¾ cup peeled, seeded, and chopped tomato

Combine all ingredients except chopped tomato in a saucepan. Bring to a boil; reduce heat, and simmer, uncovered, 20 minutes, stirring often. Stir in tomato; simmer 10 minutes. Serve with beef or chicken. Yield: 1½ cups.

PER TABLESPOON: 10 CALORIES (9% FROM FAT)
FAT 0.1G (SATURATED FAT 0.0G)
PROTEIN 0.2G CARBOHYDRATE 2.3G
CHOLESTEROL 0MG SODIUM 4MG

Chunky Southwestern Chili Sauce

TANGY BARBECUE SAUCE

Vegetable cooking spray
1¼ cups minced onion
½ cup minced celery
1 cup reduced-calorie ketchup
2 tablespoons vinegar
2 tablespoons lemon juice
1 tablespoon low-sodium Worcestershire sauce
1 tablespoon honey
1 teaspoon dry mustard
¼ teaspoon pepper

Coat a medium saucepan with cooking spray; place over medium-high heat until hot. Add onion and celery; sauté until tender.

Stir in ketchup and remaining ingredients. Reduce heat to low, and cook 20 minutes, stirring occasionally. Use for basting meat or poultry while cooking. Yield: 1½ cups.

PER TABLESPOON: 10 CALORIES (9% FROM FAT)
FAT 0.1G (SATURATED FAT 0.0G)
PROTEIN 0.1G CARBOHYDRATE 2.1G
CHOLESTEROL 0MG SODIUM 7MG

BASIC WHITE SAUCE

1½ tablespoons all-purpose flour
1 cup skim milk, divided
¼ cup instant nonfat dry milk powder
1 tablespoon reduced-calorie margarine
¼ teaspoon salt

Combine flour and ¼ cup milk; stir until smooth. Combine flour mixture, remaining ¾ cup milk, milk powder, and margarine in a small saucepan; stir well. Cook over medium heat, stirring constantly, until mixture is thickened and bubbly. Remove from heat; stir in salt. Yield: 1 cup.

PER TABLESPOON: 19 CALORIES (24% FROM FAT)
FAT 0.5G (SATURATED FAT 0.1G)
PROTEIN 1.3G CARBOHYDRATE 2.3G
CHOLESTEROL 1MG SODIUM 61MG

MUSTARD-HORSERADISH SAUCE

Add 1 tablespoon spicy brown mustard and 1 tablespoon prepared horseradish to Basic White Sauce. Serve with beef or poultry. Yield: 1 cup plus 1 tablespoon.

PER TABLESPOON: 19 CALORIES (24% FROM FAT)
FAT 0.5G (SATURATED FAT 0.1G)
PROTEIN 1.3G CARBOHYDRATE 2.3G
CHOLESTEROL 1MG SODIUM 71MG

SHERRIED MUSHROOM SAUCE

Coat a small nonstick skillet with vegetable cooking spray; place over medium-high heat until hot. Add ⅓ cup chopped fresh mushrooms; sauté 3 to 4 minutes or until mushrooms are tender. Add cooked mushrooms, 1 tablespoon dry sherry, and ¼ teaspoon dried tarragon to Basic White Sauce. Serve with beef or poultry. Yield: 1¼ cups.

PER TABLESPOON: 17 CALORIES (21% FROM FAT)
FAT 0.4G (SATURATED FAT 0.1G)
PROTEIN 1.1G CARBOHYDRATE 2.0G
CHOLESTEROL 1MG SODIUM 49MG

CURRANT-MUSTARD SAUCE

1 cup reduced-calorie apple spread
½ cup frozen orange juice concentrate, thawed and undiluted
2 tablespoons Dijon mustard
1 teaspoon grated orange rind
¼ teaspoon ground allspice
¼ cup currants

Combine first 5 ingredients in a small bowl; stir with a wire whisk until well blended. Stir in currants. Let stand at room temperature 30 minutes. Serve with pork or lean baked ham. Yield: 1½ cups.

PER TABLESPOON: 20 CALORIES (5% FROM FAT)
FAT 0.1G (SATURATED FAT 0.0G)
PROTEIN 0.2G CARBOHYDRATE 4.5G
CHOLESTEROL 0MG SODIUM 37MG

Currant-Mustard Sauce

Spicy Cranberry Sauce

1 (16-ounce) can jellied cranberry sauce
2 tablespoons prepared horseradish
2 tablespoons honey
1 tablespoon lemon juice
2 teaspoons Worcestershire sauce
½ teaspoon ground red pepper
1 small clove garlic, minced

Combine all ingredients in a saucepan; stir well. Bring to a boil; cover, reduce heat, and simmer 5 minutes. Serve warm with pork, shrimp, or chicken. Yield: 2 cups.

Per Tablespoon: 28 Calories (6% from Fat)
Fat 0.2g (Saturated Fat 0.0g)
Protein 0.1g   Carbohydrate 6.5g
Cholesterol 0mg   Sodium 10mg

Jalapeño-Fruit Sauce

Use this spicy sauce as a condiment for Buffalo Steaks on page 91.

Vegetable cooking spray
1½ teaspoons vegetable oil
⅓ cup chopped purple onion
2 tablespoons minced garlic
2 tablespoons minced jalapeño pepper
2 cups chopped fresh apricots
2 cups chopped fresh plums
⅓ cup lemon juice
⅓ cup honey
3 tablespoons low-sodium soy sauce
2 teaspoons curry powder
2 teaspoons ground allspice

Coat a saucepan with cooking spray; add oil. Place over medium heat until hot. Add onion, garlic, and pepper; sauté until tender. Stir in apricots and remaining ingredients; bring to a boil. Reduce heat; simmer 35 minutes, stirring occasionally. Serve with pork. Yield: 3 cups.

Per Tablespoon: 19 Calories (14% from Fat)
Fat 0.3g (Saturated Fat 0.0g)
Protein 0.2g   Carbohydrate 4.2g
Cholesterol 0mg   Sodium 25mg

Horseradish-Yogurt Sauce

¾ cup plain nonfat yogurt
¾ cup nonfat mayonnaise
3 tablespoons grated fresh horseradish
2 tablespoons lemon juice
1 tablespoon Dijon mustard
½ teaspoon sugar
½ teaspoon ground red pepper

Combine all ingredients in a small bowl, stirring well. Cover and chill thoroughly. Serve with beef. Yield: 1½ cups.

Per Tablespoon: 18 Calories (5% from Fat)
Fat 0.1g (Saturated Fat 0.0g)
Protein 0.4g   Carbohydrate 3.9g
Cholesterol 0mg   Sodium 214mg

Citrus Salsa

2 oranges, peeled, seeded, and chopped
½ teaspoon grated lemon rind
½ teaspoon grated lime rind
½ small lemon, peeled, seeded, and finely chopped
½ small lime, peeled, seeded, and finely chopped
¼ cup chopped green onions
1 tablespoon sugar
1 tablespoon chopped fresh cilantro
2 tablespoons unsweetened orange juice
2 tablespoons rice vinegar
1 teaspoon seeded, minced jalapeño pepper
⅛ teaspoon salt

Combine all ingredients in a small bowl. Cover and chill at least 2 hours. Serve with beef. Yield: 5 (¼-cup) servings.

Per Serving: 44 Calories (0% from Fat)
Fat 0.0g (Saturated Fat 0.0g)
Protein 0.8g   Carbohydrate 11.2g
Cholesterol 0mg   Sodium 60mg

Citrus Salsa

Fresh Peach Salsa

Fresh Peach Salsa

3½ cups diced peeled peaches (about 2½ pounds)
¼ cup diced red onion
2 tablespoons finely chopped fresh cilantro
1 tablespoon minced seeded jalapeño pepper
2 tablespoons rice vinegar
1 teaspoon lemon juice
1 garlic clove, minced

Combine all ingredients in a bowl, and stir well. Cover and chill. Serve with pork tenderloin. Yield: 14 (¼-cup) servings.

PER SERVING: 22 CALORIES (4% FROM FAT)
FAT 0.1G (SATURATED FAT 0.0G)
PROTEIN 0.4G   CARBOHYDRATE 5.6G
CHOLESTEROL 0MG   SODIUM 1MG

Colorful Herb Salsa

1½ cups diced plum tomato
½ cup diced sweet red pepper
½ cup diced sweet yellow pepper
¼ cup minced shallots
¼ cup chopped fresh cilantro
1 tablespoon minced jalapeño pepper
1 tablespoon chopped fresh tarragon
⅛ teaspoon salt
2 tablespoons balsamic or sherry vinegar
2 cloves garlic, crushed

Combine all ingredients in a bowl, and stir well. Cover and chill at least 30 minutes. Serve with grilled beef, pork, seafood, or burritos. Yield: 10 (¼-cup) servings.

PER SERVING: 15 CALORIES (12% FROM FAT)
FAT 0.2G (SATURATED FAT 0.0G)
PROTEIN 0.6G   CARBOHYDRATE 3.2G
CHOLESTEROL 0MG   SODIUM 33MG

Tomatillo Salsa

(pictured on page 128)

1 cup husked, diced tomatillos
¼ cup diced sweet red pepper
¼ cup diced sweet yellow pepper
¼ cup diced onion
1 tablespoon sugar
2 tablespoons white wine vinegar
1 tablespoon unsweetened orange juice
1 tablespoon lime juice
1 tablespoon lemon juice
2 teaspoons chopped fresh cilantro
½ teaspoon ground cumin
¼ teaspoon ground red pepper

Combine first 4 ingredients in a large glass bowl, stirring well. Add sugar, vinegar, orange juice, lime juice, and lemon juice, stirring well. Stir in remaining ingredients. Cover and chill at least 2 hours. Serve salsa with unsalted tortilla chips, beef, pork, or chicken. Yield: 7 (¼-cup) servings.

PER SERVING: 20 CALORIES (18% FROM FAT)
FAT 0.4G (SATURATED FAT 0.0G)
PROTEIN 0.4G   CARBOHYDRATE 4.8G
CHOLESTEROL 0MG   SODIUM 4MG

Did You Know?

Salsa is the Spanish word for "sauce." Salsas generally have a south-of-the-border flavor and are made with fresh ingredients and usually some form of "fire." Salsas really heat up when that fire is Anaheim, serrano, or jalapeño peppers. The fresh ingredients can range from crunchy corn to sweet peaches to juicy red tomatoes. Combine these with zesty herbs and seasonings for tantalizing flavors.

GOLDEN GARDEN RELISH

5 cups finely shredded cabbage
2 cups chopped banana pepper
1 cup chopped onion
1 cup thinly sliced celery
½ cup finely chopped sweet red pepper
2 cups white vinegar
¼ cup sugar
2 tablespoons dry mustard
1 teaspoon ground turmeric
¼ teaspoon salt
¼ teaspoon ground white pepper

Combine first 5 ingredients in a large bowl; toss. Combine vinegar and remaining ingredients in a saucepan; stir until well blended. Bring to a simmer over medium heat. Pour over vegetable mixture; toss well. Let stand at room temperature 20 minutes.

Spoon into hot sterilized jars, leaving ½-inch headspace. Cover at once with metal lids, and screw on bands. Chill at least 3 days before serving. Serve with beef or pork. Yield: 9 half-pints.

PER TABLESPOON: 5 CALORIES (18% FROM FAT)
FAT 0.1G (SATURATED FAT 0.0G)
PROTEIN 0.1G   CARBOHYDRATE 1.1G
CHOLESTEROL 0MG   SODIUM 6MG

MANGO CHUTNEY

12 whole cloves
8 whole allspice
8 whole cardamom seeds
2 (3-inch) sticks cinnamon, broken
3 cups peeled, chopped fresh mango
1 cup coarsely chopped onion
⅔ cup firmly packed brown sugar
½ cup golden raisins
1 tablespoon peeled, minced gingerroot
2 jalapeño peppers
2 cloves garlic, minced
1½ cups cider vinegar

Place cloves, allspice, cardamom, and cinnamon sticks on a piece of cheesecloth. Bring edges of cheesecloth together, and tie securely.

Combine mango and remaining ingredients in a nonaluminum saucepan; stir well. Add spice bag. Bring to a boil. Reduce heat; simmer, uncovered, 1½ hours or until thickened, stirring occasionally.

Remove and discard spice bag and peppers. Transfer mixture to a bowl; cover and chill. Serve with pork or poultry. Yield: 2¼ cups.

PER TABLESPOON: 34 CALORIES (3% FROM FAT)
FAT 0.1G (SATURATED FAT 0.0G)
PROTEIN 0.2G   CARBOHYDRATE 9.1G
CHOLESTEROL 0MG   SODIUM 2MG

Use cheesecloth to make a spice bag for simmering with the mango mixture.

Cook the chutney mixture over low heat until very thick, stirring occasionally.

Remove the spice bag and jalapeño peppers before chilling the chutney.

Mango Chutney

Sweet Tomato Chutney

SWEET TOMATO CHUTNEY

4 cups peeled, seeded, and chopped tomato
2 cups chopped unpeeled Granny Smith apple
1 cup chopped onion
½ cup raisins
½ cup firmly packed brown sugar
½ cup cider vinegar
½ teaspoon dry mustard
¼ teaspoon salt
⅛ teaspoon ground red pepper

   Combine all ingredients in a large saucepan; bring to a boil. Reduce heat, and simmer, uncovered, 1 hour and 30 minutes or until thickened, stirring often. Serve with pork or chicken. Yield: 16 (¼-cup) servings.

PER SERVING: 62 CALORIES (4% FROM FAT)
FAT 0.3G (SATURATED FAT 0.0G)
PROTEIN 0.7G   CARBOHYDRATE 15.8G
CHOLESTEROL 0MG   SODIUM 44MG

CREOLE MUSTARD

¾ cup flat dark beer
½ cup firmly packed brown sugar
½ cup finely chopped green pepper
1 (2-ounce) can dry mustard
1 tablespoon dried onion flakes
1 tablespoon cider vinegar
1½ teaspoons garlic powder
1½ teaspoons no-salt-added tomato paste
½ teaspoon pepper
⅛ teaspoon salt

   Combine all ingredients in a medium saucepan. Bring to a boil, stirring constantly, over medium-high heat. Remove from heat, and cool completely. Serve as a sandwich spread or with pork or chicken. Yield: 1½ cups.

PER TABLESPOON: 35 CALORIES (26% FROM FAT)
FAT 1.0G (SATURATED FAT 0.0G)
PROTEIN 0.9G   CARBOHYDRATE 5.8G
CHOLESTEROL 0MG   SODIUM 16MG

INDEX